Yemaya

The Ultimate Guide to the Mother of All Orishas in Yoruba and Santería

© Copyright 2023 - All rights reserved.

The content contained within this book may not be reproduced, duplicated, or transmitted without direct written permission from the author or the publisher.

Under no circumstances will any blame or legal responsibility be held against the publisher, or author, for any damages, reparation, or monetary loss due to the information contained within this book, either directly or indirectly.

Legal Notice:

This book is copyright protected. It is only for personal use. You cannot amend, distribute, sell, use, quote, or paraphrase any part of the content within this book without the consent of the author or publisher.

Disclaimer Notice:

Please note the information contained within this document is for educational and entertainment purposes only. All effort has been executed to present accurate, up-to-date, reliable, and complete information. No warranties of any kind are declared or implied. Readers acknowledge that the author is not engaging in the rendering of legal, financial, medical, or professional advice. The content within this book has been derived from various sources. Please consult a licensed professional before attempting any techniques outlined in this book.

By reading this document, the reader agrees that under no circumstances is the author responsible for any losses, direct or indirect, that are incurred as a result of the use of the information contained within this document, including, but not limited to, errors, omissions, or inaccuracies.

Your Free Gift
(only available for a limited time)

Thanks for getting this book! If you want to learn more about various spirituality topics, then join Mari Silva's community and get a free guided meditation MP3 for awakening your third eye. This guided meditation mp3 is designed to open and strengthen ones third eye so you can experience a higher state of consciousness. Simply visit the link below the image to get started.

https://spiritualityspot.com/meditation

Table of Contents

INTRODUCTION 1
CHAPTER 1: WHO IS YEMAYA? 3
CHAPTER 2: THE MOTHER'S WISDOM IN MYTH AND LORE 12
CHAPTER 3: YEMAYA AND VIRGIN MARY 21
CHAPTER 4: HOW TO CONNECT TO YEMAYA 30
CHAPTER 5: THE GODDESS OF THE OCEAN AND THE MOON 40
CHAPTER 6: RITUAL TOOLS AND SYMBOLS 52
CHAPTER 7: BUILDING A HOLY SHRINE 63
CHAPTER 8: SPIRITUAL BATHS AND SPELLS 71
CHAPTER 9: SACRED DAYS AND FESTIVALS 83
CHAPTER 10: DAILY RITUALS TO HONOR YEMAYA 92
CONCLUSION 102
HERE'S ANOTHER BOOK BY MARI SILVA THAT YOU MIGHT LIKE 104
YOUR FREE GIFT (ONLY AVAILABLE FOR A LIMITED TIME) 105
REFERENCES 106

Introduction

Human beings often tend to give identities, names, and faces to any natural and supernatural forces they encounter to better understand them and to make them more relatable. In Yoruba tradition, these forces or spirits are known as Orishas. While some people confuse Orishas with gods, they should more likely be considered spirits or deities. They are supposed to be the intermediaries between mankind and the celestial forces of the universe.

According to Yorubaland myths, Orishas were brought into this world by Oludumare. Most myths surrounding Orishas and Yoruba history take place in a region of West Africa that encompasses many rivers. The names of these rivers resemble those of the Orishas, which is why many Orisha deities originate from these rivers as guiding river spirits. One of these river spirits, if not the most crucial, is called Yemaya, also known as the Orisha of the sea.

While each Orisha is deemed equally important and is worshiped and celebrated by many people from Yoruba culture, Yemaya (or Yemoja) is one of the most worshiped Orishas in Yoruba culture. This book will thus go into great detail about Yemaya, mother of all and queen of the sea. To fully understand a deity, you need to learn the various practices and rituals associated with them. However, before you can go on to practice the various rituals associated with an Orisha, you must learn about the myths associated with them.

Particularly when it comes to Yemaya, there are innumerable stories and legends which have been passed down in Yoruba and Santeria families for centuries. Each of these stories has spiritual lessons that will make you feel closer to the wondrous goddess and help you learn valuable life lessons. Many people compare the goddess Yemoja with the Virgin Mary, which can be observed by several arguments.

There is limited literature that details the history, mythology, practices, rituals, offerings, and charms associated with each Orisha, especially Yemaya. Unlike other books about the Orisha, this book will include not only the interesting stories associated with Yemaya but also her likes and dislikes, charms, offerings, and specific prayers. To truly call upon the power of Yemoja, you'd need to fully appreciate her many aspects and create a unique relationship with her. To do this, you need to equip yourself with every bit of information about the goddess of the sea.

Overall, the devotees and initiates of Yemoja often consider her to be a compassionate, gentle deity. However, there are so many more aspects to her which should be recognized by her followers to truly connect with her divineness. As you will see in the upcoming chapters, there are many layers to the goddess of the sea. You'll also be able to learn about the various offerings you can present her with and how you can properly pay homage to her legendary existence. You don't have to practice every ritual provided in the book, only the ones that resonate with you and allow you to feel Yemaya's divine presence.

Chapter 1: Who Is Yemaya?

Yemaya is a significant Orisha, venerated in several religions such as Yoruba, Santeria, Candomblé, Umbanda, and Haitian Vodou. She is the daughter of Olodumare, the creator of the universe and the chief god of the Yoruba and Santeria religions. Yemaya is the Orisha of motherhood and sea and the mother of all Orishas. Followers of Yoruba and Santeria believe that she is responsible for all life on Earth since she is the Orisha of seas, and water is what sustains and nourishes all living creatures.

Yemaya is the Orisha of motherhood.
This file is licensed under the Creative Commons Attribution-Share Alike 2.5 Generic
https://creativecommons.org/licenses/by-sa/2.5/deed.en
https://upload.wikimedia.org/wikipedia/commons/9/9d/Yemaya-NewOrleans.jpg

Although Yemaya is highly revered in many religions, this chapter will focus on her role in the Yoruba and Santeria religions.

The Yoruba Religion

The Yoruba religion originates from West Africa, mainly Nigeria. According to their mythology, Olodumare (or *Olorun*) is the chief deity and the creator of the universe. This deity doesn't conform to a specific gender and is referred to using the pronoun "they." After they created the universe and the Orisha, there was only water and the sky. Obatala, the sky father, felt that the universe was lacking, so he asked Olodumare for permission to create dry land. They granted Obtala his request, and with the help of other Orishas, Obatala gathered the required tools and descended to Earth. He created hills and valleys and planted palm trees. Obatala spent his time on Earth enjoying the world he built, but after some time, he became lonely and required company. He asked permission to build human beings and for Olodumare to breathe life into them, which they obliged. However, Obatala was drunk when making mankind, and his creation was extremely flawed. When he woke up the next day and discovered what he had made, he was consumed with regret and vowed never to drink again.

Spiritual concepts and traditional practices govern this religion, such as Fate or Ayanmo. The Yoruba people believe that mankind must experience their destiny. Part of each person's "Ayanmo" is to become one with the divine since he is the creator of the universe and, thus, the source of all energy. This unity is referred to as "Olodumare." Before birth, every spirit chooses its destiny, who it will fall in love with, where it will be born, its career, and how its life will end. However, when a person is born, they forget everything they planned for themselves and spend their lives trying to find and achieve their forgotten destiny. Everything one thinks, says, or does, and all our interactions with one another, have one purpose; to meet and achieve one's spiritual destiny.

Another concept is the Ajogun, which is similar to the idea of the devil or a demon in the west. They are responsible for all misfortunes that befall mankind, such as diseases or accidents. One should never try to communicate with Ajogun, as they should be avoided at all costs. The Yoruba people don't believe in the devil. The concept of good vs. evil doesn't exist in their religion. No one can be all evil or all good. Human beings and morals are more complicated than that. Ashe is another concept that refers to a force that exists in all human beings, deities, nature, and even names and blood. It resembles the concept of chakras or Chi.

The Yoruba people don't consider death the end of the soul's journey. They believe in a concept similar to reincarnation, where the spirit experiences a rebirth in various physical forms. Unlike other religions, reincarnation is a positive experience that rewards good people. Bad individuals who cause harm and suffering aren't reincarnated.

The Orishas in the Yoruba Religion

Olodumare is the most powerful being in Yoruba, but they aren't involved in the lives of mankind and can't hear their prayers. They created the Orishas, who are second in the religious hierarchy after Olodumare. They are supernatural entities who act as intermediaries between the deity and mankind. They are involved in people's lives and assist them in their daily tasks by providing guidance and enlightenment. There is a misconception that the Orishas are deities. There are different types of Orishas. Some of them are demigods who were created before mankind and assisted Olodumare in the creation of the universe. They can also be the spirits of the ancestors who had an impact on the world with their good deeds and heroic actions.

There are about 401 Orishas in the Yoruba religion. Each is associated with specific powers, colors, animals, and offerings. The Orishas and mankind have a mutually beneficial relationship where human beings present offerings to appease them and ask for favors and protection. At the same time, the Orishas accept these offerings and bestow blessings in return. Both need each other to survive. People still worship and invoke these spirits to ask for their assistance. If one wants to communicate with an Orisha, they require Eshu's permission first, who stands guard at their doorway. These spirits take the form of various elements of nature, such as trees and rivers. The Yoruba people believe that whenever a misfortune befalls someone, an Orisha is angry with them and must be appeased.

The Orishas have human-like qualities. They feel happy, sad, envious, and angry. According to mythology, they rebelled against Olodumare and tried to kill him. They believed that he was getting old and they were more worthy to rule the universe since they were more involved in mankind's affairs. However, Olodumare found out and punished them.

There are seven Orishas who are referred to as "The Seven African Powers." They have the biggest number of devotees and are the most involved in people's lives.

1. Yemaya, the Orisha of the sea and motherhood, and the mother of all Orishas.
2. Obatala, the sky, Orisha, and the protector of the disabled.
3. Eshu, the Orisha of trickery and the messengers between the Orishas and mankind.
4. Shango, the Orisha of thunder, lighting, and war.
5. Ogun, the Orisha of healing and strength.
6. Oya, the Orisha of rebirth and transformation and the guardian of the dead.
7. Oshun, the Orisha of love and fertility.

Yemaya in the Yoruba Religion

Yemaya is also spelled Yemaja, Yemoja, Yemonja, and Yemalla and is referred to as "the Queen of the Sea." Her name means *"the mother whose children are fish,"* which can imply that she either has many children (like fish) or many worshipers due to her generosity. She is the Orisha of rivers, oceans, and seas and one of the most powerful spirits in the Yoruba religion. Yemaya is among the oldest children of Olodumare. She is married to her brother Aganyu, the Orisha of volcanoes, while different legends mention that she was married to other Orishas like Obatala, Ernile, and Okere. She is the mother of the Orishas Shango, Oya, Ogin, and Oshun. However, some people believe that she never had children of her own but raised many Orishas like Dana and Shango. She resides in the sea. According to the Yoruba religion, life began from her because she is water. Yemaya is the secret behind existence; without her, all life on Earth would perish.

For a long time, Yemaya was only the Orisha of the river. Her association with the ocean came later when enslaved people came from Africa to the new world. She couldn't leave her people alone, so she came with them, thus becoming the Orisha of the ocean. Yemaya is very popular among the people of Yoruba and the most beloved among the Seven African Powers. She loves all her worshipers dearly, and most of them are females. Hence, she has become the protector of all women. She represents a motherly figure with whom many of her devotees associate and form a close connection. However, just like all Orishas, she can get in the way of her followers. Invoking Yemaya at sea can be dangerous. She is a good Orisha who would never harm anyone on purpose. However, she wants to keep everything and everyone dear to her at sea. She can forget that her followers need to live on land, and she takes them when they approach her domain.

As the Orisha of motherhood, Yemaya is the most nurturing Orisha. She always comes through for her people as she cares for and protects all of them. She shares the same personality as that of her domain, the sea. She is generous and giving but can be ruthless when angry, just like the sea. When someone disrespects her or brings harm to any of her children, Yemaya brings floods and tidal waves. Beyond that, she is usually calm and patient and rarely gets angry.

She is depicted as a good-looking young woman in a blue dress with seven skirts, each one representing the seven seas. Or as a very beautiful mermaid. She wears jewelry from the sea, like pearls, crystals, and corals. She puts tiny bells on her clothes and hair that make noise whenever she moves. Yemaya causes waves by simply walking and swaying her hips. She is associated with the number seven, which represents the seven seas. She is drawn to the colors white and blue, and her favorite animal is the peacock. Everything that exists in the sea is associated with her, like shells and fish. Legends say she has long breasts because she has nursed many children. Other Orishas mocked her appearance, which affected her self-esteem. She even transformed into a river to escape their judgment.

People invoke Yemaya when they are suffering or experiencing grief, as she can cleanse their pain with her motherly love. Women struggling with infertility issues also seek her help since she has the power to heal them. Yemaya is sympathetic, listens to all her devotees when they are struggling, and comes to their aid. Women suffering from self-esteem issues invoke Yemaya as well to help them love themselves. Whatever issues women face, such as pregnancy issues, parenting problems, or when their children are in danger, they always go to their protector Orisha for help.

As the oldest Orisha, people have been worshiping Yemaya for centuries. When enslaved Africans came to the new world, more people became aware of the Orisha in North and South America.

Santeria

Santeria is a Spanish word that translates to *"devotion of the saints."* It is also called *La Religión Lucumí,* which is Spanish for "The order of Lucumí," and *La Regla de Ocha,* which means "The order of the Orishas." These names are more popular among practitioners than the name Santeria. It is often considered an Afro-Cuban religion that reached countries like the U.S., Cuba, Haiti, Brazil, and Puerto Rico through the slave trade. When Africans arrived in the Americas, they weren't free to practice their religious beliefs, as most people were Catholics. However, Africans held onto their faith to preserve their identity and as a form of rebellion. They practiced their religion in private. They passed down their traditions orally from one generation to the next. After the Cuban revolution, people wanted to be free to practice Santeria, but the Cuban government didn't trust this religion and accused its followers of practicing witchcraft. It was outlawed for a very long time, but it has recently been acknowledged, and people can now legally practice it.

Even when it was illegal, Santeria was very popular and spread all over Cuba. About 80% of Cubans follow the religion or practice some of its traditions. It is believed that Cuban's former president Fidel Castro was a Santeria follower.

Many people think that Africans and Cubans combined Santeria with Catholicism to become one faith, but this is a common misconception. The Afro-Cubans practice both religions due to the similarities between them. Some of them practice Catholicism and go to church while also practicing Santeria and going to temples. They also link the Orishas to Catholic saints. Santeria came to be from the combination of the Yoruba religion and Catholicism. Although they are different, they found similarities in their stories or personalities. For instance, Yemaya is associated with the Virgin Mary, Ogun is associated with Saint Peter, and Shango is associated with Saint Barbara. The origin of this association goes back to the time of slavery when enslaved Africans were punished for practicing their faith, so they pretended to honor Catholic saints instead. This resulted in the overlapping between the two religions and the association between the Orishas and the saints. This adds to the complexity of Santeria.

Santeria has borrowed from various cultures and religions worldwide, like Yoruba, Catholicism, and Caribbean tradition. Many of these beliefs and traditions contradict each other. Yet, the Afro-Cubans have found elements they can incorporate into their beliefs.

The followers of Santeria also believed in the supreme deity Olodumare and that he was the creator of the universe. They also believe that there is good and evil in each person and Orisha. By doing good things, you ensure your actions align with your destiny. Ashe also exists in Santeria. The followers believe that Ashe comes from Olodumare and exists in all beings and aspects of nature. Thus, Ashe is sacred, and nature is revered.

The Orishas in the Santeria Religion

Santeria, similar to Yoruba, mainly focuses on the relationships between people and the Orishas. Worshipers connect with the spirits through mediumship, sacrifice, divination, and initiation. The Orishas provide them with guidance, wisdom, success, and protection. Santeria devotees appease the spirits by presenting offerings and carrying out rituals like drumming and dancing in the hope the Orishas will assist them in achieving their destiny. They also act as messengers between the supreme deity and mankind. Only priests (babalawos) and priestesses can communicate with the Orishas through rituals, divination, and possession. Possession in Santeria (also called *mounting*) isn't a negative or forceful experience like demonic possession. When Orishas are called on during ceremonies, they mount a willing attendee, which is usually the priest or priestess leading the ritual. People can interact with the Orishas and ask them for help or advice. The Orishas also help followers of Santeria with their magic practice.

Good deeds and bad luck are associated with Orishas. Devotees believe that the Orishas are so powerful that they can perform miracles, but when they are angry with someone, they will suffer from bad luck and must acknowledge the Orishas by presenting offerings to appease them. Orishas and human beings need each other. Although they are demigods, Orishas are mortals and could die without people's offerings, sacrifices, and devotion.

The Orishas' mythology is referred to as Patakis. The Santeria practitioners are aware that these legends aren't based on facts. However, the lessons behind these stories and personal interpretations make these myths significant.

Santeria followers worship all 401 Orishas, but only a handful play a big role in the religion.

- Chango, the Orisha of sexuality and masculine energy
- Elegua (Eshu) is the messenger between Orishas and mankind
- Oya, Orisha of the dead and a warrior
- Babalu Aye, the Orisha of healing and referred to as the father of the world
- Yemaya, the Orisha of motherhood

Yemaya in the Santeria Religion

Yemaya's role in Santeria is similar to that of Yoruba. She is the Orisha of the seas and is responsible for maintaining life on Earth. She isn't the Orisha of the whole sea or ocean but only the parts known and accessible to mankind, where there are fish, plants, etc. The deeper parts of the oceans and seas belong to the Orisha Olokun. Yemaya is also associated with motherhood. Her worshipers know they should avoid angering her at all costs because her punishments can be severe. However, she quickly forgives once a person repents for their mistakes. She is a very smart Orisha and is known for her courage. She never shies away from a battle. As a protective mother, she would go to war in her children's place with a machete and defeat all her enemies.

She is often depicted wearing a long blue dress with white and blue ruffles and a belt. The color and design of the dress symbolize the waves. Her necklace is made of transparent crystal and blue beads in a pattern of her favorite number, seven. Her favorite scent is verbena, and she is associated with Saturday. Yemaya has all the qualities of a loving mother, including virtue and wisdom. However, she has a fun side as well and enjoys dancing. Her dance moves are choreographed as she starts with graceful and slow moves and then swirls while moving her skirt.

Yemaya is an expert in divination, which she learned from her husband, Orula. Back then, women weren't allowed to practice divination, so Yemaya had to spy on her husband to learn. She was so talented and a fast learner that he helped her to practice using cowrie shells. Nowadays, priests and priestesses of Santeria perform divination using the same shells as well.

Yoruba and Santeria share more similarities than differences. Both religions center on the worship of the Orishas. These entities are responsible for everything on Earth, and mankind would be lost without their constant guidance and protection. People don't only worship the Orishas because they want something. In fact, it is a sign of disrespect to only go to them to ask for a favor. Devotees should regularly express their gratitude to the Orishas for all the blessings they bestow upon them. Each person also identifies with one or more Orishas since they have human qualities which make it easy to sympathize with them and relate to their struggles.

The role and impact of Yemaya are the same in both religions. She is highly revered and loved among all her devotees. She is a nurturing mother who one can go to with any problem, and she will meet them with love and affection. There is still more to learn about Yemaya. This chapter is only the beginning. In the next chapter, we will focus on all the interesting stories that feature the Orisha of the sea.

Chapter 2: The Mother's Wisdom in Myth and Lore

There is a popular saying in Africa that *God created man because he likes stories.* Indeed, mythology has always been the cornerstone of many religions. These stories aren't just for entertainment. They explain various practices and traditions so you can better understand your faith. Stories about Yemaya showcase her personality and shed light on why she is one of the most worshiped Orishas. Wise and nurturing, there is so much one can learn from the myth and lore about Yemaya.

Stories passed down through generations allow us to understand more about Yemaya.
https://unsplash.com/photos/6jYoil2GhVk

The Birth

Santeria and Yoruba followers passed down their myths and legends orally. Therefore, there can be contradictions or different interpretations of the same stories. One version of the myth of creation shows Yemaya's role in birthing the first human. She was pregnant, and one day her water broke. Since she was one of the most powerful Orishas in the world, this event brought one of the greatest floods the universe had ever witnessed. It resulted in the creation of rivers and streams. Afterward, she gave birth to the first human. The proud mother gave her first human child a very special and personal gift. It was a seashell that carried her voice so the child could always hear its mother.

Yemaya gifted her first human child a seashell that carried her voice.
https://unsplash.com/photos/cNtMy74-mnI

Yemaya's voice still echoes to this day. When you hold a seashell to your ear, it isn't the sound of the ocean that you hear. Yemaya's voice provides her children with serenity and reminds them that their mother is always there.

A different version of this creation myth involves Orungan, Yemaya's son, with her husband, Aganju. Orungan was an aggressive, angry, and rebellious teenager. He developed feelings for his mother, which drove him to try and kill his father. Yemaya was so broken-hearted by her son's dangerous and unstable behavior that she hid on a mountaintop. She was consumed with pain and anger, and since she was known to be ruthless when her temper flared, she constantly cursed her son. One day, her cursing worked, and Orungan died.

No mother can ever tolerate the pain of losing a child, even if she is furious or disheartened with him. Yemaya's heart was so full of regret and grief that she could not handle the sorrow and died. After her death, fourteen Orishas came out of her body. Holy water was released from her womb, creating the first water on Earth, the seven seas.

Moral Lesson

Whether Yemaya gave birth to the first human or not, she was still the bringer of life on Earth by creating water. Yemaya's giving nature is also apparent in this story, as even in death, her blessings never ceased. This story showcases Yemaya's motherly, caring, loving side. Although her son committed horrendous acts and tried to kill his father, she still couldn't live without him. Just like any mother, she could never hate her son.

All mothers can learn from Yemaya's loving nature. She could have given her child gold or any expensive gift fit for a demigoddess. However, she chose something that reflects her love for her child. Who wouldn't want to hear their mother's soothing sound whenever they are hurting or struggling? Some parents can be obsessed with the material aspect of life and forget that their children could be struggling, and all they need is their soothing voice reassuring them that everything will be okay.

The Tidal Waves

Olokun is the Orisha of great wealth. He is very powerful and worthy of great admiration and reverence. However, Olokun felt that he wasn't getting the respect he deserved. This hurt his ego, and he was adamant about punishing humans to teach them a lesson. He ordered the water to send powerful tidal waves to drown everything on Earth. The ocean obliged and sent large waves to invade the lands. The people were terrified as they saw the enormous waves approaching and ran for cover.

The Orishas weren't happy with Olokun's actions – as he was destroying mankind and Olodumare's creation. They were put on this Earth to protect and assist mankind, not to cause havoc. The Orishas agreed that they must interfere and end Olokun's reckless and dangerous behavior. They went to Orunmila, the Orisha of wisdom and knowledge, to help them devise a plan. He suggested that they seek the help of Ogun, the Orisha of metal and iron, who was also a fierce warrior. Ogun told them he would design a long metal chain they could use against Olokun.

Meanwhile, the people sought the help of their protective mother, Yemaya, since she was the Orisha of the upper level of the ocean while Olokun was the Orisha of its lower level. They asked her to intervene and save them from imminent doom. Yemaya didn't hesitate and immediately took action to help her children. Before she headed to Olokun, she went to Ogun and took the chain. Standing tall like the fierce mother she was with the metal chain in her hand, Yemaya prevented the ocean waves from reaching her children.

Olokun went to meet Yemaya when he learned that she was waiting for him. Using her wise and caring nature, she calmed Olokun down, and he ordered the ocean to retreat. When the water receded, it left behind many treasures like corals and pearls as gifts for the people. Yemaya saved mankind.

Moral Lesson

There are various ways Yemaya could have handled this situation. For instance, she could have used her powers and attacked Olokun to teach him a lesson. However, Yemaya decided to use her wisdom and soothing nature to end this attack. This story teaches us that violence should never be the answer. One must always use their heart and mind. Thinking of positive solutions and approaching the situation with understanding and compassion can change its outcome.

The Slap

Yemaya was one of the most beautiful Orishas, but she had one flaw which affected her self-esteem: Yemaya only had one breast (in other legends, she had two very long breasts). She was only focused on this flaw, which made her very insecure about her looks. Yemaya believed that she would never find someone to love her. She gave up on romance and marriage. Ogun was madly in love with her, and in his eyes, she was perfect. He wanted to make her happy and prove his feelings for her. Ogun decided to impress her with his cooking skills and make her favorite dish. As he was preparing the meal, Ogun accidentally broke one of Yemaya's pots. She was furious, and they ended up having a serious confrontation. Ogun was angry at Yemaya's reaction, and he lost his temper and slapped her. She was shocked and furious, and she disappeared without giving him a chance to say or do anything else. However, Yemaya wasn't going to let him get away with his aggressive behavior without punishment. Before disappearing, she took a piece of his power, leaving him fuming angrily.

Moral Lesson

This is a story about domestic violence. Even though Yemaya suffered from self-esteem issues and believed she was unlovable, she didn't tolerate this behavior, allow Ogun to lie, or make up an excuse for his inexcusable actions. Yemaya also showed courage by taking a piece of Ogun's power. She didn't allow this abuse to go unpunished.

Yemaya's devotees usually seek her advice on domestic violence issues because she gives women the courage to handle abusive husbands. Every domestic violence victim can learn from Yemaya's story. The best reaction to physical abuse is walking away because no explanation or excuse can make this behavior acceptable. Her reaction inspires all women who look up to her and invoke her for protection and strength.

The Marriage of Shango

Shango was having an affair with Oya, who was his sister and his brother Ogun's wife. This created discord between the two brothers. Their father, Obatala, was displeased by their situation and worried their conflict would impact the kingdom. He advised Shango to get married and settle down. Shango was a womanizer, and Obatala wanted him to focus on his work and mend his relationship with his brother. Obatala suggested Shango marry his sister Oba, who was in love with him, and Shango obliged because he believed this was the only way to protect their kingdom. When Shango saw Oba, he was smitten by her beauty and kindness and found her to be the perfect match for him. They wed, and Oba proved herself to be perfect for her new role as a queen. However, there was a green-eyed monster lurking from behind.

Shango's first lover Oya was jealous and adamant about getting him back. Even though Oya loved her sister and saw how happy she was with Shango, she wasn't backing down. She was consumed with anger and wanted to unleash her wind to destroy the kingdom. However, her love and respect for her father, Obatala, prevented her. She was hurt and lonely, so she turned to the one person she trusted the most, her mother, Yemaya.

She confided in her mother about her feelings and asked for help. Oya suggested they use their powers of wind and water to destroy the marriage. Yemaya calmly and patiently listened to her daughter express her feelings. However, she was shocked to see her daughter in this condition, angry and jealous. She couldn't believe that Oya wanted to destroy her sister and the man she claimed to love. Yemaya was a strong woman and a feminist, even before the concept existed, so she was also bewildered at her daughter's willingness to start a war over a man.

Yemaya refused to be a part of this plan. Shango was her favorite son. She would never harm him or destroy his marriage. Yet, she sympathized with Oya and was sorry to see her in pain. She tried talking to her and helping her see that this wasn't the solution. Yemaya wanted her daughter to be reasonable, accept that Shango was married, and move on. She was hoping that Oya would listen to her as she always did. Both mother and daughter had a close bond, and Oya respected her mother and always sought her guidance. However, things were different this time, and nothing would be the same from then on.

Oya wouldn't be reasoned with, and for the first time in her life, she didn't take her mother's advice. Yemaya told Oya that she would protect her children against anyone who wanted to harm them. Oya made it clear to her mother that she was prepared to fight to win her lover back. From that day on, they grew apart, and their relationship never recovered. Yemaya loved her daughter very much, and it pained her that their relationship had fallen apart. However, she was still a mother, and her duty was to protect all her children, so she decided that she must stop Oya. Yemaya is an Orisha who protects and creates. She could never tolerate chaos and destruction, especially to any of her Orishas. After Oya calmed down, she realized that going into battle with her sister would make her mother angry – and Yemaya could be unstoppable when she lost her temper. She decided that the only way to win Shango back was by befriending the enemy, her once beloved sister Oba.

Moral Lessons

Yemaya's wisdom is apparent in this story. She handled her daughter's wrath with compassion and reason instead of being cruel and heartless. Yemaya was unyielding, refusing to hurt one child to please another. Oya thought her mother took Shango's side over hers, which could seem like that to some since Shango was her favorite child. However, a different interpretation of this story would suggest that she was protecting Oya from herself. She didn't want her daughter to give in to her jealousy and do something she would later regret. One should always follow Yemaya's footsteps when dealing with tough decisions, especially with family. Being calm and collected while not giving in to your feelings can be the best approach in these situations.

Duty Over Love

Yemaya fell in love with Arganyu, and they got married. They were together for many years, and their union benefited the Earth and mankind. Yemaya felt there was still more she could do to benefit the world. Still, she couldn't achieve anything new while married to Arganyu. However, she couldn't just abandon the man she loved dearly. She decided to find someone to fulfill his sexual needs and help him forget about her. No one was more perfect for this role than her daughter Oshun, the beautiful Orisha of love.

Yemaya visited Oshun, who was very happy to see her mother. However, she had a bad feeling since her mother rarely visited anyone and looked sad and anxious. Oshun knew Yemaya would ask her something, and before she could speak, her faithful daughter fell on her knees as a sign of her respect. She told her that she accepted whatever her mother asked of her. Yemaya was proud of her daughter's loyalty. She kept looking at her beautiful face and thinking she had made the right choice. Yemaya told Oshun her proposal, and her daughter was shocked.

Oshun never imagined her mother would ask her to marry her husband. She found herself in a tough position after she had already agreed to her mother's request. Oshun didn't want to disrespect her mother by refusing. Yemaya, happy that her daughter was on board, made a plan for Oshun to seduce Arganyu.

Yemaya prepared to execute her plan. She took Arganyu to Oshun's home, pretending it was a regular visit. Oshun was dressed for the role. She was so mesmerizing that Arganyu could not take his eyes off her. Yemaya signaled to her daughter that she would leave them alone to carry out the rest of the plan. Before she left, Yemaya hugged her husband tightly. Arganyu knew something was wrong, and he understood that his wife was saying goodbye. Yemaya always favored her duty and the kingdom above everything else, and he had always admired this about her. Both lovers parted ways. With every step she took away from him, he could feel his heart breaking little by little. Yemaya was devastated to leave the man she loved, but for the sake of the Orishas and the kingdom, she had to give him up.

Moral Lesson

It's a tale as old as time, sacrificing love for the greater good. Yemaya loved Arganyu, but she had to leave him to focus on the kingdom and her Orishas. She could have explained to him that she couldn't abandon her duties and must leave. However, she opted for a less cruel option by finding him someone to love so he wouldn't be alone. Giving up love for duty is one of the hardest choices anyone could ever make. Yemaya made it without hesitation, even when her heart was breaking, which shows her brave and selfless nature.

Oshun's reaction to her mother's request reflects how Yemaya was loved and highly revered among all her children.

The Road to Divination

Yemaya needed some time to be alone to recover from the pain of giving up the man she loved. As she pondered her decision, she heard a voice speaking to her. She followed the voice, and it led her to a very large tree. She found a man sitting by the tree. It was the master of divination, Orula, who asked her to be his wife. Yemaya felt bad for him. He seemed lonely and wanted to be loved. She realized that marrying could benefit them both. She would provide him with company while he taught her about divination.

They got married, but it didn't last long. She wasn't in love with him, and she still couldn't forget Arganyu. She learned so much from her new husband that she began practicing divination herself. Orula never taught her anything, but she watched him practice and was able to learn fast due to her intelligence. She was practicing in private without her husband's knowledge. People would go to her everywhere to tell them about their future. They were impressed by her talent and would talk about this great diviner until the news reached Orula.

Unaware that it was his wife, Orula was curious about this new diviner. He asked around until he found her. Yemaya was doing her readings at the tree where they first met. She was surprised to see Orula, who felt hurt and betrayed. He ended their marriage on the spot. She was grateful for her time with him and the things she had learned. This time, Yemaya wasn't heartbroken because she was not in love with

Orula. Arganyu was still in her heart, lingering on her every thought.

Moral Lesson

Marrying Orula out of pity shows how kind-hearted Yemaya was. She didn't want to see a poor soul alone and suffering. Her purpose wasn't only to learn from him and change his life for the better. This story also shows how big her sacrifice was, as she still couldn't forget about the man she loved. Her intelligence also came through here in how she didn't require someone to explain to her how divination worked. She learned everything just by observing and became one of the greatest diviners of all time.

Yemaya was brave, intelligent, selfless, loving, caring, wise, strong, and a mother. Her stories help us understand her not only as a supernatural being but as a woman, a human who loves and feels pain. They are filled with lessons one can learn from and incorporate into daily life. Yemaya is worthy of being an idol to all women. The mother, lover, protector, and feminist, Orisha is an admirable character that is worthy of being highly revered.

Her actions also teach us that change is necessary and nothing stays the same. You can grow and transform when you welcome change with love and compassion. Yemaya is the protective mother who exists in all her children. One should always turn inward and seek her protective spirit and endless love.

Chapter 3: Yemaya and Virgin Mary

In several African Diaspora religions, Yemaya is syncretized with the Virgin Mary, the Catholic saint with similar characteristics. She is also known as the Virgin of Regla and Our Lady of the Sea - a portrayal that's more accurate to Yemaya's divine nature than the spirit of a saint. This dedicated chapter discusses the connection between Yemaya and the Virgin Mary and how this syncretism came to be. You will learn how Yemaya is worshiped as a saint and how the depiction of the Virgin Mary relates to the portrayal of Yemaya as a Yoruba Orisha.

The Virgin of Regla.
*Christian Pirkl, CC BY-SA 4.0 <https://creativecommons.org/licenses/by-sa/4.0>, via Wikimedia Commons
https://upload.wikimedia.org/wikipedia/commons/e/e7/Virgin_de_Regla_Cuba_001.jpg*

What Is Syncretism?

In order to comprehend how the image of Yemaya became associated with the Virgin Mary, you must first understand what syncretism is and why it happens. The term syncretism depicts the fusion of religious ideas rooted in two or more different belief systems. Religious beliefs can only be accepted if they are based on thoughts people are familiar with. Consequently, it can be concluded that all religions have syncretism. For example, the idea of the creator or God (or gods) was only accepted because it helped explain events people already considered as deeds of a higher power. Once a religious thought becomes a belief, it can be interpreted in many ways. How these sentiments are interpreted and diversified over time shapes the cultural and traditional evolution of the different belief systems. Sometimes, syncretism only causes religious systems to adopt new ideas. On other occasions, it leads to the formation of new belief systems. A classic example of the latter is Santeria, the African Diaspora religion which syncretizes African deities with Catholic saints.

During the Transatlantic slave trade, thousands of Africans were brought to the New World, where they were forced to convert to Christianity. Their indigenous pagan practices were banned, and they were expected to be devoted to saints instead of deities. However, followers of the Yoruba religion soon realized that saints had much in common with the gods and goddesses of the Yoruba pantheon (the Orishas). This made it easier for them to accept saints as patrons but also allowed them to keep venerating the Orishas. They renamed the Orishas to the names of the saints with similar characteristics and started worshiping them as saints. Some consider this false syncretism since the Orishas were only masked with the name of the saints. In some religions, like in Santeria, this can be true. After all, the practitioners of Santeria didn't fully convert to Christianity; they just pretended that they did. Then again, in countries like Cuba, Yoruba deities are worshiped as Orishas and saints, which alludes to at least partial acceptance of Catholic beliefs.

Other fully-syncretic religions contain elements that come from contradictory sources. Voodoo and Hoodoo, for example, incorporate segments of Christian beliefs, African spirituality, and African folk magic practices. Magic and Christian beliefs couldn't be further from each other, yet these religions make them work together naturally. Religions such as Judaism, Islam, or Christianity aren't considered syncretic - although historically, they have been known to draw elements from each other.

The Connection between Yemaya and Virgin Mary

Now that you've learned what syncretism entails, you can explore why Yemaya has been syncretized with the Virgin Mary and not any other Christian saint. In Yoruba, Yemaya is viewed as the Orisha of the seas and a warrior goddess. She is also the divine mother to the human race, embodying the most powerful feminine force in the universe. She is the champion of defenseless children and mothers, empowering them. Yemaya nurtures maternal values and promotes love and peace amongst humans - in their personal life and in their communities. She can also contribute to the balance of the family by keeping children safe and ensuring the family's economic well-being is secured so the children can thrive.

As one of the most prevalent figures in Christianity, Mary is viewed very similarly to Yemaya. She is a symbol of purity and motherhood. Not only is she the mother of a son who had a tremendous role in shaping the belief system, but Mary is also the motherly figure of all human beings. She is known for having a loving and nurturing nature, both towards her son and the rest of humanity. Always ready to help those in need, the Virgin Mary is a source of spiritual empowerment and the patron saint of mothers, children, and families.

While Yemaya is known for her fluid nature (she is a water goddess, after all), she is a generally good-natured Orisha. She can be angered, especially if someone disrespects her or her protegees. However, she can be easily appeased with offerings and other acts in her favor. Mary is always depicted as a serene woman who calmly expresses her faith in her son and the rest of humanity. She is more of a silent protector than Yemaya, who isn't afraid to voice her opinion as needed. Their syncretization in Santeria and other diasporic religions helped reconcile the differences between these feminine divine aspects. Mary became stronger while staying true to her calm protective nature. In contrast, Yemaya remained the fierce patron of mothers and families while gaining the ability to resolve situations more calmly.

Yemaya and the Virgin Mary teach their followers to believe in themselves and live purposefully. They intercede on behalf of mothers and children. They also help those who struggle to keep their families happy, healthy, and secure. This is particularly true for Yemaya because, as an Orisha, she can relay messages people can't convey otherwise. She carries these messages to Olodumare, the supreme creator and spiritual guide. While Mary's interference is more subtle, she still provides strength for overcoming obstacles. In some religions, Oludumare is called Olofi and is syncretized with the Holy Spirit in Christianity. The Virgin Mary is associated with the Holy Trinity, which also connects her to the Christian version of Olofi. In syncretized religions, Olofi is the patron of worldly affairs and communicates with Orishas/saints. Depending on the specific interpretation, Olofi/the Holy Spirit can also be addressed by people.

How Is Yemaya Worshiped as a Saint?

Yemaya has a rich history of being worshiped as an Orisha, as known from the rich oral history of the Yoruba. Her actions are immortalized in the repositories of the wisdom collected by the Yoruba ancestors. These vessels of knowledge can be accessed by modern generations, and this is how present-day practitioners have found their connection to the Yoruba deities, including Yemaya. The beliefs surrounding Virgin Mary have a similarly long history. While she is rarely mentioned in the New Testament, she is referenced several times in the Old Testament. African Diaspora religions have a much shorter past. Still, the element of Yemaya's syncretization as a saint has left its mark on the cultural background of these religions and their devotees. Just like the Yoruba offered prayers, rituals, and personal sacrifices to Yemaya, so do the practitioners of African Diaspora religions with her person as a saint.

Amongst the Cuban practitioners of Santeria, Yemaya is known as the Virgin of Regla (or Our Lady of Regla), a black saint capable of materializing divine empowerment into people's lives. She is often asked to change people's disposition, allowing them to reach spiritual enlightenment and have a balanced life. She can also help dispel negative influences and transform one's life by encouraging them to take a positive approach. Yemaya - as a saint - can be asked these favors by individual people who make small offerings and prayers to the saint regularly. When the inquiry is more significant, it requires a ritual performed by a priest or priestess, just as it's done in the parental religion. However, unlike in Yoruba, Yemaya - as a saint does - not need to provide her ashe (spiritual essence) to the devotees. She bestows her blessing, provides guidance, and does whatever she is asked for without any spiritual possession.

The Virgin Mary has several forms, including Mary, Star of the Sea, and Our Lady of Rule. In Santeria, Yemaya (again, as a saint) is associated with both. She is revered as Our Lady of Rule (Virgin of Regla) for her identity as the Mother goddess. Santeria's followers give her just as much prominence as the Catholic Church. She is offered prayers on Saturdays, observed in visions during meditation, and is expected to perform miracles when invoked. Mary, Star of the Sea, represents the ultimate fusion of Yemaya and saint. She possesses both the Sea goddess's power and the Virgin Mary's nurturing nature. She is also honored on Saturdays. Expecting mothers pray to her for safe delivery and healthy children, while those wanting children ask her to bestow the gift of fertility. Those wanting a safe journey overseas will also pray to her before departure.

Lone practitioners and people who want to keep a strong connection to this saint pray to her daily. Here is a typical prayer that followers of syncretic religions offer to Yemaya as a saint. It's known as the Pagan Hail Mary. It is recited by facing a large body of water (sea or ocean) or at the altar while looking at a small bowl filled with saltwater. It goes like this:

> *"Hail Mary, the embodiment of grace,*
> *You are enlightened.*
> *You are blessed among women,*
> *and so is the fruit of your womb.*
> *Hail Mary, mother to us all,*
> *Bless your children now and throughout their lives."*

Santeria practitioners often use a rosary as well when praying to Yemaya/Mary. If you are comfortable with this, you can also try repeating several Hail Marys while going through the beads. Start with a few and slowly expand your focus until you can recite an entire rosary of prayers. The prayer can also be said before meditation and other practices dedicated to Yemaya.

When they're finished with the prayers, followers typically ask the saint for guidance or any other form of intercession they need from her.

This works if Yemaya knows what your problem is. If you're asking her a favor, provide a clear description of your issue.

Celebrating the Virgin of Regla

Santeria and other syncretized religions aren't centralized, nor do they have assigned places for worship. Rituals in the name of Mary and other saints are held at the home of the high priests and priestesses. Eventually, they can be hosted at a place of importance for the local community. A great example of this is the procession of the Virgin of Regla. It celebrates Mary in her aspects as Our Lady of Regla. The procession is held every September seventh between the docks of Regla (entry point for Havana) and the Church of Our Lady of Regla, located nearby. Worshippers gather near the church to venerate the saint patron of Havana and the sea. They wear layered dresses in colors of the sea – blue, azure, turquoise, and white – and carry white flowers. They also wear colorful necklaces made of flowers and beads.

Priests and priestesses express their devotion by carrying white candles and holding traditional beaded bracelets. Apart from these devotees who worship Yemaya as an Orisha (masked as a saint), some venerate her as a saint, holding the symbol of the Virgen de la Regla and crucifixes. Some (typically the latest generations) try to respect both sides by exhibiting symbolic behavior. As they walk toward the church, they cross themselves in the name of Mary (a Catholic tradition) and offer coins to Yemaya (a Yoruba custom). Around them, dancers are moving in a floating motion. They wear a blue skirt made of several layers (seven is the traditional number after the number of seas governed by Yemaya) and a white blouse. As they dance, they simulate the movement of the sea, accentuated by the color of their clothing, which makes them look like they're foaming waves.

Until recently, they danced to the traditional Yoruba drum rhythms called bata. Due to the overlapping motives in the different faith systems, the traditional drummers quit supporting the procession of saints. Now, the dancers and the devotees are accompanied by simple, newer forms of music authentic to Cuba.

When they enter the church, devotees of the Virgin make their way to the large statute elevated in honor of the saint. There, they lay flowers and say a quick prayer to her, expressing their gratitude and wishes. Some wish to spend a few private moments with the Virgin. After everyone has paid their respect to the Virgin, a traditional Catholic mass is held. Then, everyone leaves the church, carrying the statue with them. They walk towards the dock, crossing seven "windows" made of a wooden construction adorned with flowers and icons of the Virgin. The dock of Regla has a symbolic significance for many devotees. It opens to a waterway that connects Cuba to Florida and the Atlantic Ocean. It was also the first place the freshly enslaved Africans set foot in the New World during the transatlantic slave trade. At this place, devotees feel a deeper connection to their roots and ask the Virgin to help them keep these memories alive. After this, they sing a few traditional songs devoted to Mary. They turn the statute towards the water, so she can admire her kingdom, then say goodbye to her. The statue is then carried back to the sanctuary, where worshipers can visit her, offering prayers and asking for guidance.

Devotees who also celebrate Mary as Yemaya hold a different ceremony in the evening of the same day. They use drumming and chanting, calling on the Orisha. Those devoted to the combined version of her aspects will hold séances called *misas espirituales*. As their name implies, these spiritual masses have the purpose of communicating with the saint on a spiritual level. It's also customary for the hosts to contact the souls of ancestors and spiritual guides. The souls of former slaves who, in their time, also venerated Yemaya or the Virgen de la Regla are also called upon.

The Depiction of Virgin Mary

In art, Virgin Mary is depicted very similarly to Yemaya. She's wearing a serene expression while sitting or standing in her kingdom. However, there are several distinctions between the portrayals of Yemaya and the Virgin Mary. Notably, the saint is surrounded by clouds, watching over her children. Meanwhile, Yemaya is often depicted as standing in or over water, overseeing her kingdom and making it safe for travelers. Another difference is that while Yemaya is typically dressed in blue, Mary is seen wearing a white dress and a blue cloak or veil. Her white dress reflects her virginal status, which is in stark contrast to Yemaya's passionate nature. With the blue veil, Mary retained some of Yemaya's symbolism, which alludes to her status as a patron of the seas. It also gives her an allure of purity, as water is considered one of the most powerful cleansing agents.

Mary wearing blue isn't present only in the new, syncretized religions. It's referenced in the Old Testament, where Mary is compared to the Ark of the Covenant, a sacred relic protected by a blue cloth. This reference stems from the description of Mary carrying her son shrouded in Heavenly protection. In Christianity, the color blue is the symbol of the sky. When used in clothing (especially a piece reflecting modesty like a veil or cloak), the color blue means the person is protected by the Heavens. Mary (with her blue veil) is blessed for her devotion to all her children. It shows that she is a radiating female force who uses her power subtly and only when asked to do so.

Mary's blue veils also give her a distinguished status. Historically, blue and purple have always been associated with royalty and other people in good material standing. Until the invention of artificial dyes, clothes were colored with natural agents. This made blue fabric extremely hard to create and so expensive that only the richest members of society could afford them. Mary is always depicted as a modest woman. However, her blue veil indicates that she wasn't lacking anything (at least not in what's truly valuable, such as moral riches). That said, unlike Yemaya, who is typically portrayed with a large, floating skirt made of seven layers, Mary's clothes are more modest. Her dress is long but has a simple design.

Other depictions show her as the Queen of Heavens, with a blue veil denoting her divine status. In Santeria's religious art and symbolism, she is dressed in elaborate clothes, wearing blue and white, even when referred to as Yemaya. Mary is depicted as a young white woman, just like in Christian art. Yemaya, the saint, is notably black, sometimes with water droplets shining on her skin as she has risen from the sea. In rituals, people wear both blue and white as colors of Yemaya, using these as a connection to her grace and nurturing wisdom.

Sometimes, Mary is depicted wearing all blue clothes, standing over a snake. This image symbolizes her powerful nature and refers to her defeating the snake (the devil) by crushing its head.

Chapter 4: How to Connect to Yemaya

Whether you're already familiar with Yoruba practices and traditions or just getting introduced to them for the first time, connecting with Yemaya shouldn't be seen as something very hard to achieve. The best approach to this is to properly understand the goddess's origin and the cultures, traditions, and religions she comes from. You cannot truly connect with the goddess until you've learned all about the heritage she comes from - this is essential, even when praying to the goddess, as it will convey your respect for her and the cultural practices associated with her. Moreover, the practices associated with Yemaya's worship vary widely due to unique origin points, so it's vital to learn about each religion and culture.

Connecting with Yemaya is a spiritual experience.
https://unsplash.com/photos/0chVl3b15MQ

Although connecting with Yemaya shouldn't be intimidating, it does require you to put in some effort. Like many religions, the true secrets and rituals needed to fully connect with the goddess are only revealed to the initiated. So, it's preferred that you get properly trained within one or all of the religions associated with her. Suppose you're not well-informed about the rituals that you attempt to practice. In that case, you'll only end up with an ineffective spell at best and may even risk offending Yemaya. It's also disrespectful to Yoruba practitioners and Yemaya devotees when you perform their rituals without any prior training or knowledge. Therefore, it's critical that you always approach these rituals and traditions with respect and honor. This chapter will serve as a proper guide to connecting with Yemaya and explain how you can worship her respectfully.

Connecting with Yemaya: The Basics

Let's start with the basics of incorporating various practices into your life, which will make you feel more connected to the mother goddess, Yemoja. These simple gestures and daily rituals will greatly affect your spirituality and allow you to understand your favorite Orisha more deeply. Here are a few ideas on how to incorporate the magic of Yemoja into your daily life and rituals:

- Incorporate blue and white-themed clothes and charms into your life. This way, whenever you wear the sea Orisha's colors, you'll be reminded of her.
- If you're fond of long, flowing skirts, try an outfit with some white skirts to be reminded of Yemoja.
- Yemoja devotees wear seven silver bracelets on one arm to portray their allegiance to the sea goddess.
- Practice ocean or water magic when visiting the beach, river, or lake.
- Jot down your wishes, spells, and prayers to Yemaya on a blue or white paper boat, and float it out to the sea.
- Drink more water throughout the day.
- Spend time looking at the fish at an aquarium, river, or beach.
- Do some water activities like sailing, boating, or cruising to feel the sweeping power of the ocean.

- If you've been praying to have children, include Yemaya in your fertility rituals and spells.

Symbols, Magical Attributes, and Offering

In addition to common practices used when invoking Yemaya, you can also include some symbols, charms, and magical offerings into your practices to have a better chance of forming a bond with the goddess. You can use these items on your altar or in daily rituals to attract Yemaya's energy.

- Dry sand from a beach
- Fresh water from a beach, river, or lake
- Pearls, fish, rocks, and shells found on a beach
- Fish nets
- Fountains
- Small paper or wooden boats
- White flowers
- White or blue ceramic dishes that carry fresh water from the sea or river
- Blue and white-themed charms
- The number 7
- 7 cowrie shells, 7 pennies, or 7 white roses

Most people associate Yemaya with fertility and other feminine aspects in life. However, she has much more depth than is usually observed. True devotees of the goddess know her actual value. Every Orisha she came into contact with developed their potential when she came into her full form. Yemaya shouldn't only be invoked when trying to perform fertility rituals but, most importantly, when you're planning to nurture your goals and manifest your true purpose. If you want to bring their ideas to life, Yemaya's energy will be extremely beneficial for you.

Altar for Yemaya

An altar for Yemaya can be created similar to how you'd design an altar for the element of water. For this purpose, you can choose a smaller-sized altar that you dedicate to the sole purpose of praying to the sea goddess. Before you can start practicing rituals or praying to Yemaya, you will need to cleanse this altar and bless it with positive energy.

This altar will act as a proper channel through which you can connect to the goddess and should therefore be free from any negative energy. Take a few minutes out of each day to pray to the goddess using this altar and make regular offerings in her name. Meditate on her presence at this unique altar you've created just for her (more about meditating later). When you meditate with the altar right in front of you, imagine yourself being surrounded by the goddess's pure white energy and her element of clear, blue water. Either chant to her, pray to her or play songs that remind you of her or the ocean.

While there will be a proper guide to creating an altar for Yemaya's worship later in the book, ensure you follow a blue and white theme to adorn the altar. Use sea shells, models of fish and other sea creatures, and even pictures depicting the sea goddess. Use white candles to create a luminist scene at the altar while adding some flowers as well.

Other Ways to Connect with Yemaya

As discussed before, Yemaya is frequently associated with the moon, and many of her worship rituals involve the moon cycle alignments. Therefore, a good way to connect with her would be to incorporate the moon and symbols associated with the moon into your worshiping practices and any other rituals. Secondly, Yemaya is also often associated with the number seven. She's depicted wearing seven skirts which basically represent the seven seas. Therefore, the number seven should also be included in your practices in whichever way you see fit. For instance, you could light seven white candles on your altar or arrange seven cowrie shells while you're meditating. There should be no limits to your creativity when invoking Yemaya. She is a creative spirit herself and greatly appreciates any kind of innovation and creative spirit. For instance, some people make offerings to Yemaya for seven consecutive days.

Many ancient drawings and paintings also often depict her wearing bells in her hair and clothes. Therefore, the sound and use of bells can also be associated with the goddess and incorporated into ritual practice. Another common symbol linked to the sea goddess is the peacock. So, try using peacock symbols or peacock feathers as charms on your altar. Yemaya quite often responds positively to spells or rituals done in the name of healing, protection, creativity, and self-love. However, you should avoid asking for favors if you're not leaving enough offerings for the goddess because, with Yemoja, it is a two-way street.

Ideal Offerings for Yemaya

If you want to be in the good graces of Yemaya, the trick is to be generous with your offerings. A detailed chapter will discuss the various offerings you can leave her. Make sure that you visit the ocean or some river frequently to make these offerings. While it's okay to perform the rituals at your house and pray at the altar you've created, your spells and prayers will be most effective when you're close to water.

Ideal offerings for Yemaya can include sea shells, salt water, charms, flowers, fruits, herbs, and even food items. The best way to show reverence for her is to leave offerings that speak to her personality traits and associated elements. You could sing sacred songs or compose a unique prayer for her. Or, you could chant her name and use the vibrations of your voice to connect with her energy. Some people even make food dishes to pay tribute to the goddess.

Other Important Aspects of Connecting/Talking with Yemaya

According to Yoruba legends, Yemaya is considered to be the queen of the ocean and the mother of all living beings. She is considered to have many offspring whom she nurtures and protects. She loves her children more than anything else and is thus very kind and generous. Therefore, you should always approach her with reverence and respect. This is especially important for people not familiar with Yoruba practices and traditions. Suppose you feel interested in connecting with Yemaya. In that case, it's important that you first take the time to study the lore, traditions, and culture associated with her. You should remember that connecting with the Orisha is not something to be taken lightly and requires a lot of effort. Therefore, you need to always be respectful of the relationship you form with an Orisha deity.

Yemaya Meditation

Meditation is one of the most popular methods used to connect with Yemaya.
https://unsplash.com/photos/2pUP1Ts1bmo

Meditation practice is considered to be one of the best ways of connecting spiritually with an Orisha. Meditation helps ground you, cleanse your energy, and aligns it with the deity you favor – if done correctly. To practice meditation to connect with Yemaya, follow these steps:

1. Find a quiet, comfortable place in your house away from all sorts of distractions. Light seven white candles and place them in front of you (take care of fire safety). Use an oil diffuser or incense to create the perfect meditation environment.

2. Close your eyes and let your body relax. Take three slow, deep breaths, and set your intention for the meditation sessions. Open up your heart to Yemaya's energy, and chant in your mind, "I want to connect to Yemaya/Yemoja."

3. Now, imagine that you're on a beautiful island, completely surrounded by the deep blue ocean. The sky above is free of clouds, with the sun shining brightly. Feel the fresh, cool breeze on your face and enjoy the view.

4. Imagine playing in the water, splashing around in the cold, fresh waves. Now think about getting on a small boat, letting the

current take you out to sea. Focus on the feelings you have when surrounded by the ocean. Instead of feeling scared of the vastness of the sea, you'll feel at ease.

5. Envision the energy around you changing suddenly. You start to feel loved, cocooned in warmth, and look up to see a beautiful woman rising out of the sea. She looks at you and says, *"I am the Sea Goddess, Yemaya, Mother of all. I'm pleased that you have connected with me. Come with me, and let me show you who I am."*

6. After this, imagine her taking you into her arms and into the sea. While you're with her, ask her questions and for blessings. Once you've finished connecting with her, say your goodbyes, take three deep breaths, and open your eyes.

7. Once you're back in your room, go over everything you've learned about her, and memorize how you feel right after the meditative session.

8. When trying to connect to Orisha deities, make sure you use the Orisha's name to invoke their presence. In this case, Yemaya's sacred name is Aquamarine, and her sacred water is Blue Agate. Also, make sure to use the goddess's name when presenting offerings to her.

Given below are some additional tips for connecting with Yemaya.

- To make meditative sessions more interesting, sit near a lake, river, sea, or even swimming pool and immerse your legs inside. The water will act as a conduit between you and Yemaya. While practicing this, you can also wear a flowing white skirt, which will sway around your legs when you're in the water, giving you a mermaid-like look.
- Another way you can better connect with Yemaya during these meditative sessions is by wearing a seashell. Seashells are her symbols and will make you feel her presence more strongly. You could also hold the seashell in your hand or near your ear to be able to hear the goddess.

Prayers for Yemaya

Stay in the good graces of the sea goddess by praying to her regularly, either in daily rituals, at occasional festivals, or in front of her altar.

Prayer 1:
> Yemaya, oh blessed queen of the seas,
> Let the sacred waters of the ocean wash over me.
> Hold me, oh mother, your child.
> Cleanse my soul, nurture my life, and sustain my spirit.
> Yemaya, oh, magnificent one.
> You who wear the seven sacred skirts of the seven seas,
> Move around me and surround me with your energy
> To wash away all negativity
> Oh, Yemaya, mistress of the tides and the moon,
> Bless me with your sacred light,
> and fill me with your energy.
> Help me to complete my purpose.
> Oh Yemaya, healing ocean mother,
> I ask you to fill me with your cleansing energy.
> Bless me with your pure waters,
> And let me heal with its regenerative energy

Prayer 2:
> Strange clouds and fragments of beauty.
> Envisioning shining stars of a story.
> Invoking you among the goddesses of the waters.
> You calm the storm with your joy.
> You bring calm with your kind words
> The sea breeze brings your energy to us,
> Oh, goddess of the sea and rivers
> You kiss the beautiful moon
> and bless us with your waves
> The waves carry beautiful flowers.
> Hidden in the waters.
> Their aromas are the hope that makes you
> the Goddess of the Ocean.

Prayer 3:

    I sense the comfort and love of a mother as I gaze at your picture. I know you are close, guarding and directing your children. I lower my head in admiration and respect; I ask you for your graces. May God grant you permission to purify my soul and body with your divine waters, and may my Earthly path be illuminated by your divine light. Amen

Prayer 4:

    Bring blessings and fortune to those who are in need, O magnificent Yemaya. We hope, dear Mother, that through your graces, we will achieve what we ask for in this prayer. Although we know that, due to our shortcomings, we do not merit what we ask for, we implore you to answer our prayers. Amen.

Prayer 5:

Queen who is Mother of All,

Goddess of the Ocean Depths,

defender of women

Ensure people are aware of your presence all over this holy place.

We who pray to you as Yemaya,

Our Mother, Our Womb of Formation,

ask that your love keeps rolling and washing over us

as the ocean waves, as the creeks from your breasts.

Yemaya, Mother of the Fish,

You who are solace, encouragement, and redemption,

We call you forth to enter our hearts and souls.

Prayer 6:

You are the force that ripples underwater,

She who binds the sea and the sky, the eternal mother who reclaims you.

Feel the sand under your toes, press the conch to your ear, and gaze upon my blue,

and you know Me.

Submit your problem to Me,

Toss your worries into the ocean's core that is Me.
I'll take care of you, dry your tears, soothe your anguish
and shield you from the upcoming storms.
In your submission, I embrace your voice.
In the giving over, I become your liberty.
Daughter, return home and allow me
to make unified
everything that is fragmentary.

Prayer 7:

You who control the waters, pouring over humanity your protection, O Divine Mother, wash their bodies and their thoughts, performing a purging with your water and ingraining in their soul the regard and reverence due to the force of nature that it symbolizes. Let us safeguard your group of things and what they protect.

We beg strong Yemanja, Queen of the Waters, to receive this plea.

With goodness and love, give me the necessary capacity to withstand everything.

In your ocean of beauty and tranquility, I desire to live.

Keep my loved ones safe from harm and peril.

All hail Yemanja, Sea Queen!

Yemaya is considered to be one of the major Orisha deities mentioned in Yoruba legends. She is the mother of all and is thus easy to seek and connect with. Her spirit is nurturing and warm, which makes her entity all the more attractive to people. Yemaya devotees and worshippers are present worldwide and have different ways they pay homage to the Goddess of the Sea. People often seek her blessings and wisdom when they desperately need healing and protection in their lives. While many sources have mainstreamed the worship of Yemaya, her actual reverence stems from unique cultures and practices not known by many. For non-native devotees, it is incredibly hard to find authentic sources to understand how to properly connect with the goddess. The techniques provided in this chapter will hopefully help you connect more thoroughly with Yemaya.

Chapter 5: The Goddess of the Ocean and the Moon

The tides and the moon have always been interconnected. The water gravitates toward the moon, and it spins and turns with the moon's phases. Traditionally, Yemaya is seen as the goddess of the ocean and the moon. However, the public only acknowledges her rulership over water bodies. It fails to recognize or remember that she governs the moon as well.

Yemaya is also known as the goddess of the ocean and the moon.
https://unsplash.com/photos/8Gl7Ew-q6D8

The goddess Yemaya has many faces and a few reincarnations. In the beginning, when the oceans and the moon were first created, Olokun appeared and announced himself as the owner of the water's depths. He then dived into the water and created a splatter that evaporated into the skies. Immediately, the skies began to rain, and the droplets returned to the ocean. This was the moment when Yembo, the first incarnation of Yemaya, appeared. Yembo declared that her kingdom is "where the moon touches the waters."

Yemaya's full name is Ye Emo Eja, which directly translates to "the mother whose children are as numerous as the fish." It is believed that Yemaya gave birth to both the sun and the moon, as well as the first fourteen Orishas.

This chapter's main focus will be on Yemaya's connection with the moon. This includes various rituals that are done on certain moon phases as well as different prayers and spells that relate to the goddess and your connection with her.

Yemaya and the Phases of the Moon

The moon holds great power and affects everything around you, including yourself. Think of the way the moon affects the water or how most predators strike on the new moon. The moon's gravitational pull is so strong that it moves oceans and seas. It would be ridiculous to think that the moon can have this strong influence over the Earth but not affect humans in any way.

The phases of the moon affect humankind too. For instance, it is common knowledge that people's emotions are heightened during the full moon. This chapter will go in-depth about the different moon phases and what humans go through during each phase. However, before delving into the moon's phases, you need to understand Yemaya's role in all of this.

The first incarnation of Yemaya gave birth to the moon and the stars. She is the goddess of the night sky and waters. Yemaya created different moon phases to create order and harmony in life on Earth.

Every moon phase is associated with different themes in life. For instance, the new moon is linked to certain subjects, while other moon phases are associated with different themes. Why should you know this? Well, simply because the chances of receiving optimum results are higher when you pray or cast spells during relevant moon phases.

For instance, picture yourself praying for a new start. This is better accomplished during the new moon. Why? Each moon phase has powers, so asking for a new beginning will yield results during the new moon, but it will not be as powerful during a waning crescent. The waning crescent is associated with endings, so the power of your prayer and the waning crescent will clash. This is why it is better to cast spells or pray during phases that relate to what you are asking for or trying to manifest into existence.

Remember that the phases are divided into two groups: beginnings and endings. The first four phases are more about beginnings and new events, while the other four are more about endings and old situations. The full moon does not fall into either group and is considered a powerhouse by itself.

In spirituality, the moon is linked with the subconscious, intuition, femininity, fertility, magic, and psychic abilities. In Yoruban and Santerian traditions, Yemaya is also associated with these areas.

The goddess also rules over the realm of dreams. This includes prophetic and lucid dreams. This means that the goddess can respond to your calls and prayers through dreams. People who pray to Yemaya usually ask for her protection during pregnancy or ask that she help them with their fertility. Others ask her to guide their spiritual journey when they are practicing magic or casting spells. Spiritualists also ask Yemaya to guide and strengthen their intuition.

Yemaya is seen as the mother of all, so if you ever need to feel motherly love and protection, you can always pray to the goddess for just that. There are a million reasons to pray to her. It all comes down to what you need from the goddess.

If you would like to spark a connection, you should know that she responds when the time is right. This means that her response may not be instantaneous all the time. She will reply to you when you are ready to receive the answers or when the circumstances are right. She may appear in your dreams or send you direct messages that will be unquestionably from her. She will make sure that you understand that she is the sender, and the answer will be clear as the bright full moon in the sky.

New Moon

The new moon may be dark and indistinguishable from the night sky, but its powers surpass its appearance. This is the first moon phase. It brings about change, new beginnings, a new version of you, and a new page in your story. It has a child-like energy, and you will feel this enthusiasm if you connect with Yemaya during this phase.

This is the best time to bring your ideas to life. So before the new moon arrives, start a list of things you would like to begin or start with the new moon phase. When the sun sets and the moon rises, go to Yemaya's altar and invoke her.

Cleanse the altar, light the candles, and begin the invocation by saying, *"Queen of the Sea, Mother of life, I come to you this new moon night. In the reflection of your mirror, beneath your holy gaze, I give you honor, homage, and praise."*

You can use the same prayer on different moon phases; just make sure to say the correct moon phase. After your prayer, start communicating with the goddess. Share with her everything that you would like to start this month. Ask her to give you opportunities and guide you with your decisions.

During this period, if you receive invitations or come across a clear sign that the goddess heard your callings, answer them. It will be best if you do not reject invitations during this time. The goddess may send new people your way, unexpected invitations, or other opportunities that will create a path for what you want.

Waxing Crescent

The waxing crescent graces the sky two days after the new moon. During this moon phase, you will feel more confident in yourself and your abilities. You will feel a surge of bravery, making you more likely to take risks. It is essential to try to stay grounded during this phase because you might feel a bit impulsive.

This moon phase will not influence reckless or impulsive behavior, but people react to the moon differently. This means that if you are naturally impulsive, then you may feel more impulsive during this phase. If you are prone to recklessness, then consider asking the goddess to help you make wise decisions during this time.

Like the new moon, the waxing crescent brings fresh beginnings with it, but it also makes people feel more optimistic and confident enough to take on new tasks. It also weakens self-doubt, so if you are a person who second-guesses themselves a lot, you will feel more confident.

One of Yemaya's symbols is the crescent moon, so when you are praying to her during the waxing or waning crescent, make sure you have the crescent moon on the altar. When you pray to the goddess, tell her about the anxieties and fears you would like to eliminate during this time. Tell her about your new projects, but also tell her about what worries you. Ask her to give you confidence and comfort. The waxing crescent powers will give you confidence and trust in yourself, but the goddess can multiply them for you.

First Quarter

The first quarter and last quarter are known as the half-moon. In Santerian and Yoruban culture, the half-moon is a symbol of the goddess' perplexing knowledge and wisdom.

This moon phase pushes you to do better. In other words, it challenges you to overcome your fears of the unknown or the unseen. Why is that? Only the first half of the moon is visible, but the rest is not. This phase symbolizes the binary relationship and the sharp contrast between what you know and what you do not. The first quarter moon gives you strength and a deeper perspective.

During this time, you will be able to be more honest with yourself and reflect on various aspects that need to be worked on or fixed. You may feel anxious during this phase, and this is why you can burn Allspice as an offering to the goddess. This spice is used in various spells, but when it is burned on the first quarter moon as an offering, it sends your prayers to the goddess.

It is believed that burning this plant helps to reduce anxiety and stress, and it also makes you feel more relaxed. When you offer this spice to Yemaya, she will understand that you need immediate help with your fears and anxieties about the future.

You can burn this herb every first quarter moon as a ritual. Remember to cleanse the altar and invoke the goddess before you offer her any offerings.

Waxing Gibbous

The waxing gibbous moon is the last phase before the full moon. This placement makes this phase special. Why is that? Well, the full moon is considered to be the most powerful moon phase, so the waxing gibbous contains some of this power.

This moon phase brings positive opportunities and potential with it. During this time, you might feel like you are about to gain new experiences or manifest goals and dreams into reality. Trust your feelings and intuition during the waxing gibbous. If you feel like you are about to embark on a journey, you will be correct. This phase brings wealth, self-development, and successful manifestations with it.

The waxing gibbous will reward you even if you have been working for what you are trying to achieve. During this time, you can burn pine or Yemaya incense as an offering to the goddess and as a way to bless your financial gains within this period.

If you would like to add Yemaya incense to your workings, you can follow the recipe below.

Ingredients:
- Powdered star anise pods
- Rose petals
- Basil Leaf
- Powdered sandalwood
- Lemon verbena
- Meadowsweet

You will need the following:
- Dust mask
- Glass bowl
- Mortar
- Pestle

Steps:
1. Add herbs and plants to the mortar.
2. Put a dust mask on.
3. Crush ingredients with a pestle.
4. Add mixture into the bowl.
5. Pray to Yemaya over the ingredients.
6. Share with her your intentions and goals.
7. Place the bowl over Yemaya's altar.
8. Leave it there for 14 days.

9. Seal the powder in a container.
10. Burn the powder over charcoal.
11. Use during the waxing gibbous phase or when you are praying to the goddess.

Full Moon

The full moon is the most powerful of all the moon phases. This phase symbolizes the maternal figure that is Yemaya. She is considered the mother of all, and the full moon symbolizes her motherhood and all of her children.

You will be blessed with clarity and enlightenment on the first night of the full moon. You will receive emotional and mental clarity. You will not be doubting or second-guessing yourself, your choices, or your decisions. If you are feeling a bit emotional during this phase, then this is nothing to worry about. Almost everyone feels emotional under the light of the full moon. Your heightened emotions will bring you a lot of revelations. In other words, it will make you see what your subconscious may have been hiding from your conscious mind.

During this time, women are known to become more fertile, or there is a higher chance for them to conceive. If you intend to work with Yemaya during this time, then you will be very busy. There are various chants, prayers, and spells that you will be doing during this period.

If you want to work on your fertility with the goddess, then place a bowl of almonds on her altar and chant:

"*Today! Today, I'm going to sing!*
I will praise in the sand, at full moon, the mother Iemanjá!
Rose of the sea, My blue sky star, It's not a fisherman's story
That my love will give you.
He leaves! Let the waves of the sea pass.
Hear the song of the beautiful Odoiá.
I wish he sent A big love From the bottom of the sea."

Begin by eating the almonds, given that they come from a separate bowl, not from the offering. Now, you may be wondering, why should I eat almonds? Well, almonds are known to help with fertility when you are working with Yemaya. They are considered to be a magical net in fertility spells as well.

If you want to seek Yemaya's protection, the best night is on a full moon. For this spell to work, you will need to take a trip to the beach, so get ready to pack a few things with you.

Ingredients:
- Holy oil
- Yemaya oil
- 7 quartz crystals
- 7 cubes of camphor
- 7 blue votive candles
- 7 silver fish hooks
- 7 silver coins
- 7 pennies
- 7 cubes of camphor
- 7 bluing balls
- 7 glass jars
- 3 keys
- Juice of 7 limes
- Blue cloth (square)
- White towel (clean)

Walk into the water during the high tide and stop when the water reaches your ankles. Now, ask the Eleggua to open the path for you and leave 3 keys as an offering. Count 7 waves and begin chanting the following to the goddess:

> "Queen of the Sea, Mother of life, I come to you this Full Moon night. In the reflection of your mirror, beneath your holy gaze, I give you honor, homage, and praise."

When you have finished, dip the jars in the ocean and then dry them with a clean towel. Fill the jars with crystals, fish hooks, bluing, camphor cubes, and coins. Make sure to put these ingredients in the same order and chant,

> "I call the power of the sea, Keep my home safe and protect me."

Repeat the same chant every time you place 1 crystal or 1 key in the jar. When you have finished, you will have completed 35 chants.

Now, fill ⅔ of the jar with sea water and leave the pennies where the water meets the sand. When you are done, pack your jars and go home. Lay 7 plates on the ground and create a circle. Put each jar on every plate. Place the 7 candles next to the jars and anoint them with Yemaya oil. Fill your bathtub with water and add Florida water, sea salt, lime juice, and bergamot oil. Sit in the water for exactly 28 minutes. Make sure you set a timer. When the timer rings, pat yourself with a white towel. Remember to pat, and do not rinse. Put holy oil on your feet, hands, third eye, and heart.

Now, go back to the circle you created and cast an energetic spell. To do this, simply envision a white light forming a protective shield around you. Light each candle and say,

"Spirit of the sea, protect me."

Close your eyes and picture the water rising to protect you. Spend 28 minutes in meditation while keeping this image in your mind. When you have finished, say the following,

"Spirits of water, I thank you for lending your Ashé to this site. Return to your kingdom beneath the waves. Hail and farewell."

Close the circle and place your candles in random spots in your house. Do not blow them out; let the wax melt away. Store the seawater that is in the jars in another container and hang the talismans in a blue cloth. On the seventh day after the spell, pour the seawater in a clockwise motion around your house.

Waning Gibbous

The waning gibbous is the first phase of endings. This is the best time to shed away any self-sabotaging habits and self-destructive mindsets. You will likely meet parts of your shadow self during this time. When you do, do not reject these parts of you, you may not like how they make you feel about yourself, but accepting them is imperative. By accepting them, you will be releasing yourself from their tight grip.

Suppose you would like to shield yourself from your destructive habits. In that case, you might want to anoint candles with Yemaya oil on the goddess's altar or burn Yemaya oil and pray to her while inhaling the oil's sweet aroma.

Ingredients:
- 7 drops bergamot oil
- 7 drops sandalwood
- 2 drops lemon verbena
- 2 drops rose oil
- 1 oz. almond oil
- 1 pearl
- 4 drops magnolia
- Sea salt crystals

You will need the following:
- Reusable eye-droppers
- A small funnel
- Glass bottle
- Mortar
- Pestle

Steps:
1. Add almond oil to the jar.
2. Let it sit for 7 minutes.
3. Pour in the rest of the oils.
4. Use a dropper for the oils.
5. Cleanse the dropper with rubbing alcohol so you do not mix the oils.
6. Crush the pearl with your mortar and pestle.
7. Add the powdered pearl to the jar.
8. Swirl for 3 minutes.
9. Pray to the goddess for protection.
10. Add the sea salt crystal to the jar.
11. Seal the jar with its lid.
12. Leave on the altar for 7 days.
13. Use the oil for anointing yourself or candles. You can also burn the oil when you are praying for protection.

Last Quarter

Similar to the waning gibbous moon, the last quarter is also connected to the shadow self. This moon pushes you to work or fix your more negative traits or habits. It will draw your attention to the shadowy sides of you by making you confront it through friends, family, or people who are close to you.

You might be confronted with your negative habits. Do not be fazed when this happens. Try to be accepting of the situation and forgive yourself. Remember to befriend your shadow self and look at it as a pathway for your healing.

The best thing to do here is pray to the goddess and ask her to enlighten you and help you through this period with as much grace as possible. Remember that alone time is essential during this time, so grab your incense and sit by the beach. Connect with yourself and the ocean, and you will eventually feel better.

Waning Crescent

The waning crescent phase pushes you to pay attention to your needs. During this phase, you might feel exhausted. This usually happens to draw your attention to your energy levels and self-care. Suppose you have been straining yourself or spending most of your time worrying or caring for other people. In that case, this is the time to dedicate some of this care toward yourself.

Spend time by the ocean to connect with Yemaya and allow yourself to feel her love and care toward you. Make sure you meet your needs and do things that you genuinely enjoy, even if it means oversleeping or spending the whole day on the couch.

Dark Moon

The dark moon is the last phase, and it is the exact opposite of the new moon. The new moon is all about new beginnings, unlike the dark moon. During this time, you will feel nudged to end things that no longer serve you.

This is the time to cut off toxic friendships, end unfruitful relationships, or leave extremely taxing jobs. If you feel like the moon is telling you to eject a certain thing from your life, then take it as a sign.

However, you must reflect on what you are ending and your reasons for ending it. Do not end relationships or leave a job if you are unsure about your reasons.

It is best to offer a magnolia to Yemaya's altar or burn it by her altar if you want to gain wisdom during this challenging period.

Every moon phase contains power and energy that is unique to it. These energies affect you daily, whether you are conscious of it or not. However, now you know what they do and how Yemaya is connected to the moon and its phases. If you would like to work with the goddess, consider performing some spells or rituals during the relevant moon phases.

Chapter 6: Ritual Tools and Symbols

Yemaya is a generous and open-minded deity who usually accepts any kind of offering presented to her, given that the person's intentions are pure. However, it is best to present customized offerings and presents when trying to win the favor of any Orisha deity, and Yemaya is not an exception to this. Whether you present her with pearl-adorned combs, beautiful necklaces, fragrant perfumes, stunning paintings and depictions of her, flowers, seashells, stones, or food offerings, she'll happily accept your gifts and shower you with her blessings.

A lace fan is among the many offerings preferred.
https://unsplash.com/photos/ZdMg-ILt20A

Many people also leave her blue or white lace fans and feathered fans with duck or peacock feathers. As discussed before, these animals have special importance to the sea goddess. Thus any item representing them is deemed significant. Yemoja prefers small bells, fish nets, aquamarine gemstones, crystal beads, pearls, masks, and blue-colored glass – though the most popular offerings for Yemaya are observed to be food and flowers.

One of the most common symbols associated with Yemaya is conch shells. Most of her depictions portray her holding these cowrie shells. The legend associated with this symbolic item is that Yemeya would fill these shells with her comforting voice. Moreover, these shells have a narrow slit on one side, while the other looks like a pregnant belly, which connects them to the fertility goddess, Yemoja. According to legend, Yemaya fills these cowrie shells with the gift of fertility. The nurturing spirit wants all her offspring to be the most authentic versions of themselves, which is why she blesses the people on their path to find their meaning in life and pursue their dreams.

Cowrie shells are found all over the world but were considered to be sacred objects back in the day. People even used them as currency. Many women wore them as jewelry and traded them for spices and silk. These shells are incredibly versatile and are found in various shapes, sizes, and colors. As these shells were considered symbols of fertility back in the day, they were gifted to new brides or laboring mothers to ensure safe delivery. Today, many Yemaya worshippers wear cowrie necklaces and bracelets to channel their goddesses' energy. People keep the opening visible to signal their desire for a partner or might symbolize their strong opinions.

The Sacred Cowrie Shells

Since ancient times, cowrie shells have had supernatural significance in Yoruba and Santeria rituals and traditions. However, going into the full extent of those rituals is too complex to provide here. Instead, you can try a simple way to use these cowrie shells to connect with the divine. This is done by practicing a yes-no questions ritual, commonly known as Obi. There are about 5 possible answers that can be obtained from this practice. To perform the ritual, you will need 4 opened cowrie shells (the natural hump on the back of the shell should be cut off and sanded to result in a fairly flat surface). When the cut sides faces up during the reading, it means the shell is silent, whereas when the mouth-shaped side faces upward, the shell is speaking. Additionally, you'll need a simple cloth or mat to place on the ground or a table. This is where you'll be casting the shells. Make sure you pray to the spirits and ask them for their guidance before you cast the shells.

Cowrie shells have supernatural value in Yoruba and Santeria rituals.
Sodabottle, CC BY-SA 3.0 <https://creativecommons.org/licenses/by-sa/3.0>, via Wikimedia Commons https://commons.wikimedia.org/wiki/File:Cowrie_shells_-_sozhi_roll_of_3.jpg

Take the four conch shells in your hands while envisioning your question or the situation you're inquiring about. Focus solely on the question and slowly blow on the shells. Then, shake the shells in your hands, and roll them onto the mat like you would roll dice. Interpret the answers according to the following guidelines:

- If all four shells land with their mouth-shaped side facing up, it indicates that all four are speaking. This is considered a blessing, so the answer should be considered a yes. You'll be successful in what you asked about, more than you hope. You can do a second throw to see if your luck will last long.
- If three shells land with their mouth-shaped side facing upward, while one is downward, three will be speaking while one will be silent. This answer is less positive than the first one and can be considered a maybe. Although many people consider this answer a yes, the one silent shell creates doubt about the issue.

To further check for the answer, you can do a second throw. If the second throw yields all four shells speaking, then it translates to a yes. However, if you get one shell silent again, you should move on with your decision. For more than two silent shells, the answer should be considered to be no.

- If two shells land with their mouth sides facing upward while the other two are downward, this is considered a very positive response. This response tells you that everything is balanced, harmonious, and perfect. Throwing the shells a second time is not wise whenever you receive this answer.

- If you get one shell with the mouth upward and three of them downward, the silent shells outweigh the speaking ones. This is a clear no. It indicates that the thing you inquired about will be extremely difficult, if not impossible, to achieve.

- The last possible scenario is that you get all four shells facing downward or being silent. This response is an irrevocable no but is also a warning. It tells you that negative forces surround you and that you need to do spiritual cleansing as soon as possible.

Spirits and deities often commune in this pattern when called upon for guidance. However, extensive practice is required before you can master this art and interpret your answers correctly. You should make additional throws if you're not completely satisfied with your answer, but most experts suggest against more than two throws in a row.

Other Symbols and Associations

Although many of these have been discussed before, here's a list of symbols and associations connected to Yemaya which can be very helpful for your practices and rituals:

- **Days of the week** - Saturday is considered sacred to Yemaya, as discussed previously, but some stories also suggest that Friday is an important day of the week for the sea goddess.

- **Metals** - lead is the most commonly associated metal for Yemaya. It is the only metal that does not corrode easily in seawater and thus holds a special place for the sea goddess. She also accepts offerings made of silver and steel as well.

- **Colors** - the color blue holds a special place in Yemaya's heart. It is the color of the vast ocean she lives in. Different shades of blue should be used to present offerings. White is another favorite color of the goddess. It symbolizes the kindness and purity of the mother, Orisha. Some people also add green and red beads to the necklaces worn for festivals celebrating Yemaya.
- **Necklace** - beaded necklaces are common offerings for Yemaya. Her sacred necklace consists of seven white beads, succeeded by seven blue beads. This pattern is then repeated until the necklace is long enough to be worn. White beads can also be substituted by clear beads.

Floral Offerings

There's a widespread misconception that Yemaya only favors white roses as floral offerings. While it's true that white flowers are her favorites, and she does prefer roses, these are not the only varieties she likes. Yemaya loves any blue or white flowers but accepts flowers of all colors, particularly pink, yellow, red, or violet blooms. What matters the most when presenting floral offerings is the flowers' freshness, beauty, and fragrance. It's best to present them in groups of seven, if possible, to respect the goddess's sacred number. If you ever see beautiful flowers floating on the waves of the ocean, or some river, rest assured that someone else left them as presents for Yemaya. Never try to pick these flowers up or take them with you, even if they get washed up on shore.

Yemaya loves blue and white floral offerings in particular.
https://unsplash.com/photos/qzoSJlPxS9k

When presenting floral offerings to the mother goddess Yemaya, follow some guidelines to show your respect to her. Wear white flowing skirts or a dress, if possible. Let your feet soak in the water, but don't venture deeper than that. Before putting the flowers into the sea, bring them close to your heart and pray to the goddess. Ask for her blessings and guidance. At the end of the prayer, count seven waves before tossing the flowers into the sea. Wait for seven heartbeats and take seven steps backward before turning around and walking back to the beach. During this, ensure you do not turn your back toward the sea to show your respect to the goddess.

You can also make non-floral offerings at the seaside. However, make sure whatever you toss into the sea isn't toxic to marine life. Plastics are off-limits when throwing offerings into the sea. You could toss food items into the sea, but ensure you take the packaging off them first to avoid polluting.

Food Offerings

Many practitioners prepare food offerings for Orisha spirits to keep them nourished and happy. These offerings are commonly placed on their altars for a short time. People also prepare meals favored by these deities and eat them with their families to honor the Orisha. In Yemaya's case, she prefers her food offerings to be presented at the seaside if possible. You could also leave them at a lake or in a river. Yemaya is said to reign over all water, so you can make your offerings at any place convenient to you.

If none of these options are possible for you, you can always leave some food at her altar or at the roots of an old, large tree. Wherever you leave the offerings, be sure to clean up after yourself. It is essential to consider the environment when leaving out food as offerings. The food will eventually rot and degrade the environment with it. The spirits will not be offended if you let your offerings sit for a while before disposing of them responsibly.

Like every other Orisha deity, Yemaya has several food items she favors above all – which include goose, duck, ram, rooster, turtle, hen, swan, lamb, shellfish, and seafood. She also loves pork rinds, especially when freshly fried. Vegetarian offerings for the goddess can include blueberries, bananas, watermelon, seaweed, plantains, honeydew melon, cantaloupe, and lettuce. She also has a taste for scrumptious desserts filled with heavy cream and syrups. These can include cane syrup, saltwater taffy, molasses, sweets, white wine, and pound cake.

Cooking for Yemaya

While you can present ready-made food items to Yemaya as offerings, there's just something special about preparing a whole meal in the name of your favorite goddess and spiritual guide. Cooking is one of the best ways to show Yemaya how dedicated you are to her. Plus, she loves a creative spirit and will surely enjoy your attempt at making some of her favored dishes. You can either share this meal with your family or present it to Yemaya and then share it with your spiritual community.

Spicy Seafood Stew

This delicious recipe for a spicy seafood stew is savory, unique, and fits perfectly with Yemaya's personality. You can serve it with shrimp or add scallops.

You will need the following:
- 1 yellow pepper (chopped)
- 1 red onion (diced)
- 1 green pepper (chopped)
- 1 red pepper (chopped)
- ½ a stick of salted butter
- ½ lb. of clams
- ½ lb. of mussels
- 1 lb. of raw shrimp (shelled and cleaned)
- Salt and pepper (as needed)
- 1 tbsp flour
- 4 tbsp garlic (minced)
- 5 ounces oysters
- ½ cup of fish stock
- 1 tbsp of cajun (for seasoning)

Steps:
1. First, you will need to prepare the sauce. To do this, melt the butter in a medium-sized pan at high heat.

2. Once the butter is completely melted, add the onions and stir until they turn translucent.
3. When the onions are done, add the flour and mix thoroughly. Make sure there are no lumps form in the sauce.
4. The sauce will turn golden after a while, and this is when you will need to add the fish stock into the mix. Stir well.
5. Finally, add the rest of the chopped vegetables, garlic, and seasoning to the pan.
6. Let the mixture cook for about 10 minutes so that the peppers become soft. Once they're tender and soft, add the oysters to the pan and cook for another 5 minutes.
7. Next, add the clams and mussels to the mixture, and stir for 1 minute. Add the shrimp next, and cook until they turn pink and start to curl. Serve hot.

Coconut Macaroons

Don't confuse these macaroons with the fancy French delicacy most people think of, but rather sweet mounds of coconut and sugar. Almost every Orisha loves this dessert, and while it's easy to buy sweet treats from the market, baking them yourself will show a level of devotion not everyone has. Plus, these aren't that difficult to prepare and only require simple ingredients.

You will need the following:
- ½ tsp of vanilla extract
- ½ cup of sugar
- ⅛ tsp of salt
- 3 large eggs (whites)
- 14 ounces of coconut (sweetened)

Steps:
1. Preheat the oven to 300 degrees and start preparing the batter.
2. Mix the sugar, salt, and egg whites together in a small bowl until mixed completely.
3. When the egg whites start to get frothy, add the vanilla extract and then fold the batter into the sweetened coconut.

4. Use a spoon to scoop out the batter and place it onto a baking sheet in the shape of little mounds.
5. Place them in the oven, and bake for about 25 to 30 minutes. Periodically check to see if the edges have turned golden brown. That's when you'll need to remove them from the oven. Serve with caramel or chocolate sauce.

Coconut Shrimp

Coconut Shrimp.
https://unsplash.com/photos/ag8O-k-DzC0

This can easily become one of your favorite recipes and is loved by Yemaya as well. Keep in mind that this is a bit trickier than the other recipes, so if you're confused about any instructions, take a deep breath and center yourself, or ask a friend to help. These fragrant delicacies will transport you to the Caribbean beaches in no time.

You will need the following:
- ¾ cup of breadcrumbs
- ½ tsp of salt
- ⅓ cup of flour
- ½ tsp pepper
- 1 cup of coconut (shredded, sweetened)
- 1 tbsp vegetable oil

- 2 large eggs
- 1 lb. shrimp

Steps:
1. First, you need to peel the shrimp and remove all the veins, but be sure to leave the tail intact.
2. In a small bowl, mix the flour, salt, and pepper together.
3. In a separate bowl, whisk the two eggs until they start to froth.
4. In another bowl, place the breadcrumbs along with the sweetened coconut. Mix them thoroughly.
5. Now, place the bowls in sequence so that you can take the shrimp and roll it into the flour mixture first.
6. Then, dip it into the egg mixture and cover it completely. Finally, coat the shrimp with the breadcrumb and coconut mixture and place it on a plate.
7. Do this with all the shrimp, and then place them in a frying pan or skillet with medium heat.
8. Fry the shrimp for about 2 minutes on one side and another 2 minutes on the other. Remove the fried shrimp from the pan, and place them on paper towels to drain the oil.

Food offerings for Yemaya should be cooked in proper pots, pans, or ovens and then served on a sopera (the Spanish word for "tureen"). A sopera is a ritual tool dedicated to Orishas and is used to present food offerings to the deities. Each Orisha has a sopera dedicated to them, which is decorated according to their personality traits. For Yemaya, the sopera should be white in color but decorated with blue swirling, wave-like designs. You can get creative with the designs you want to paint onto the sopera or serving plate.

Tools and Sacred Objects

Ritual tools and objects hold a special power not understood by many. They are filled with the energy of specific Orisha and have quite an effect on a spell or ritual. These sacred objects symbolize deeper, hidden meanings associated with each Orisha and act similar to talismans or objects used in magic. In most Yoruba traditions, after someone is initiated into the ranks of the devotees, they are given sacred tools cast in lead. These can be used to channel Yemaya's energy when performing a ritual or spell. Below is a list of sacred ritual items you can use to channel Yemaya's Ashe, or energy, for a spell or ritual.

- Cowrie shells - tools for divination
- Full moon - symbolizes Yemaya's motherhood status
- Half moon - symbolizes Yemaya's wisdom
- Anchor - symbolizes stability
- Seven hoops or bracelets - symbolize Yemaya's wealth
- Mermaid charms - symbolize Yemaya's supernatural beauty
- Oars - represent the balance between good and evil (always in pairs of 2)

Rituals and spells are a common part of Yoruba practices and are performed throughout the culture. Symbols and ritual tools hold a special power that should never be underestimated. Making these tools a part of your practice will be highly beneficial for you. Try to get hold of the tools and charms associated with Yemaya, even if you've not been initiated into the ranks yet. However, always be respectful of the goddess and the practices you perform. Try not to disrespect any sacred objects or ritual tools particularly associated with Yemaya or, generally, Yoruba practices. Keep them situated at the altar you've created or in a cabinet somewhere. Furthermore, keep the goddess in your favor by offering her regular presents and flowers near a river or sea.

Chapter 7: Building a Holy Shrine

Although not everyone considers building a shrine a fundamental part of their practice, those who do agree that having a holy space has many advantages. Reading this chapter, you will learn about the benefits of building a shrine in or near your home and using this space to venerate Yemaya. You will be provided with numerous beginner-friendly tips for erecting a shrine to Yemaya, how to care for it, and how to use it for making offerings to the Orisha. The advice from this chapter should only serve as general guidelines. While certain elements are necessary to honor Yemaya, feel free to add your own personal touch to the space to fully empower your shrine. This will enable you to form a powerful bond with her, and she will help you achieve all your goals.

A shrine is needed for you to have a place to connect with the Orishas.
Greg Willis, CC BY-SA 2.0 <https://creativecommons.org/licenses/by-sa/2.0>, via Wikimedia Commons https://commons.wikimedia.org/wiki/File:Voodoo_Altar_New_Orleans.jpg

Benefits of Building a Shrine to Yemaya

A spiritual center for one's practice is a critical part of many pagan and non-pagan traditions. Having a sacred place dedicated to your practice has many benefits for your soul and your connection with your guides and the Orishas you worship. Below are a few of the greatest blessings you can gain by building a shrine to Yemaya.

Gaining a Place for Invoking the Orisha

Working with Orishas is a spirituality-based practice. Each item you place in your shrine becomes connected to your soul and the spirit of the Orishas you want to evoke. They represent emotions, intentions, and symbols of spiritual guides that can help you grow spirituality, access ancestral wisdom, and more. Yemaya is known for always being there for those in need. You will have a direct way of communicating with her through a shrine made in her honor. The more you use your shrine to call on her, the more spiritual power you garner throughout your practice. From the first stone you put onto the shelf to the first candle you see flickering in front of you, it will all nourish your spirit just like it's being nurtured by the mother goddess.

Water-based altar decorations, like the ones used to represent Yemaya, often include simple items that enhance the need for spiritual empowerment. Growing your connection with Yemaya involves using your shrine for several days, often placing new items on the holy surface each day. Whether you opt for exchanging the existing ones or adding new objects depends on the purpose of each individual practice. Either way, it will enhance the power of your spiritual work and deepen your connection to this Orisha. You can also share the shrine with other people. Their contribution to this common sacred space will fortify the spiritual bonds within your community. This will have a positive effect on your community's connection to Yemaya.

Inviting Plenty of Positive Energy

A shrine is a space where you can harness the goddess's spiritual energy (or ashe, depending on your religion). However, it can also be a valuable tool for inviting and retaining her nurturing energy in your home for an extended period. Yemaya has plenty of positive energy to share with her devotees. Setting up an altar or shrine for the mother goddess and taking care of it will ensure that positive energy keeps flowing through your space. It will follow you wherever you happen to be in your home.

Expressing Your Creativity

Building a shrine is an excellent way to express your creativity. While there are certain items you'll need to use, figuring out how to place them requires much creative thought, even if you have a guideline like the one provided in this chapter. You only need to learn how to take a creative approach to honor Yemaya through the shrine and how to maintain good care of it. At the same time, it allows you to build something unique and express your thoughts and emotions through your creation. Whether you honor Yemaya as an Orisha, a saint, or a goddess, you will always have several choices for venerating her and asking her for her blessings. Remember, Yemaya has many faces and can help you with different aspects of your life. She can bestow the gift of fertility in a multitude of areas, nurture your talents, grant you a safe voyage overseas, and much more. Whichever your goal is, there is a way to express it through the decorations you use for the shrine.

Replacing Negative Influences with Positive Energy

Negative experiences and influences can hinder your ability to be fertile and productive and cultivate self-love. If this is the case, Yemaya is the perfect person to turn to – and building a shrine to her is the first step in the right direction. By creating a shrine for Yemaya, you gain a space where you can do something about negative influences, regardless of their source. Whether the negativity comes from living beings or spirits, having a sacred place will empower you to fight them and keep them away from you and your life.

Learning Her Correspondences

There is no better way to learn the correspondences associated with an Orisha or saint than displaying them in a space you visit on a regular basis. And this applies not only to their colors and favorite items but to their preferred offerings too. Learning the correspondence of Yemaya will let you see firsthand how they work best. This information will help you understand what she likes and what to avoid when making offerings for her. It will allow you to form a much deeper connection with her during your daily practice.

Creating a Sacred Meditation Center

Shrines can be transformed to represent more than one Orisha or saint. However, even if you wish to dedicate your shrine exclusively to Yemaya, this space can be the perfect space for meditating with the goddess. By bringing together the right combination of elements, you can create a space where you can unwind after a busy day at work. As you evoke Yemaya's spirit and it permeates your senses, your body and mind relax, and your experience becomes deeper. If you're also making an inquiry, you can use incense and other tools known to help focus on a specific question or request. For relaxation, choose the ones that feel right to use in any situation. There is no better way to ground yourself than by meditating in front of the offerings dedicated to Yemaya, the goddess known for her calming essence and spiritually nurturing vibes.

Focusing on Your Intentions

You can call on Yemaya daily or only during the days associated with her and festivals. Either way, having a holy space can help you focus on your intent every time. Building the shrine is a great way to start focusing on whatever you want to ask the goddess. As you put things together, you leave mundane thoughts and worries behind. You're slowly transitioning into a thought process where there is only you, Yemaya, and tools that help you form a connection with her. If you practice magic with others, the shrine can bring each person's intentions or messages together and focus them toward the goddess. And if you are a solitary practitioner, you can tailor the space to your specific taste and preferences, which also helps enhance your spiritual powers.

Honoring Your Ancestors and Other Spirits

A shrine made for one Orisha (in this case, Yemaya) can also be used for seeking spiritual guidance from your ancestors and other spirit guides. Yemaya encourages you to nurture your familiar connections. This applies to both living relatives and those who are dead. You can always ask for Yemaya's guidance whenever you're in a difficult situation in life. However, don't be surprised if she tells you to turn to those who know you best - your family. Given her understanding and compassionate nature, she won't mind if you call on her and evoke your ancestors during the same ritual. You can also place offerings for her and the ancestors. Their collective wisdom can get you through even the most challenging situations. You can create a space where your devotion to Yemaya coexists with ancestral veneration. This will be a good reminder that you have several powerful forces supporting you.

Welcoming Nature

Establishing a connection with nature is another way to develop your spirituality and connection with Yemaya. Many devotees choose to grow medicinal herbs and plants for food, even if they only do this in a small corner of their home. By placing your harvest on the altar or shrine along with water, you can express gratitude for them. Some of these can be perfect for offerings - and prompt Yemaya to help you gain insight, cast a spell, or perform any other act that aligns with your traditions and culture. You will most likely leave the offerings on the altar for a number of hours and days. This allows the notice of their presence to be carried to Yemaya, and she will provide many blessings in return.

Sharing Your Devotion

Whether introducing someone to Yoruba or Santeria practices or wanting to find common ground with another devotee, building a shrine to Yemaya together can be a great way to share your spiritual beliefs. This is a common practice for celebrating her sacred days and festivals. Involving others in the building of the shrine or its preparation for the festivities is a great way to connect with your children or the children in your family/community. Yemaya has a special place in her heart for children, and nothing will make her happier than seeing them become valuable members of her community.

How to Create a Shrine for Yemaya

From where you place it to the items you put on it, there are a lot of details that go into building a shrine. Here are a few tips for creating a shrine for Yemaya in or near your home.

Shrine Placement

Before you start building a shrine, you must choose a suitable place for it, ideally in your home. However, if you'll share it with others or if you don't have space for it in your home, you can set it up near the house. This is a particularly great idea if you live near an ocean or sea, as this helps reinforce your effort for evoking Yemaya. Ideally, the shrine should be erected away from high-traffic areas or possible distractions. Otherwise, you won't be able to relax, let alone focus on your inquiry during your work. Many devotees opt for setting up their shrines in their home office or bedroom, as they spend most of their time in these rooms. Having a sacred place in your bedroom could also facilitate morning and evening prayers to the goddess, which are recommended to maintain a potent connection with her. If you don't have much space for a full table to serve as a shrine, you can always set up a smaller area on your dresser, vanity table, or even inside your closet. Alternatively, you can create a shrine on the windowsill. Leaving the door open and working under the moonlight is another excellent practice for keeping in touch with Yemaya. If you plan to practice meditation or similar techniques to communicate with the goddess, build the shrine in a room that can accommodate these activities too.

What to Use in the Shrine

Creating a shrine requires using all the items associated with this goddess. These are:

- Blue pieces of cloth - or one single piece, depending on how big the shrine will be
- Cowrie shells, or, if you can't find these, you can use any variety of sea shells
- Pearls, real ones, if possible
- A statute or picture of Yemaya
- Anything else that symbolizes Yemaya; pictures of dolphins, mermaids, waterfowl, and other sea creatures
- A sopera - a dish used for offerings made for Yemaya
- A blue gown (optional)
- A silver crown and other silver objects
- Fans
- A white candle
- A blue candle
- Incense; Yemaya incense or your favorite incense with a calming scent
- White or blue flowers or a bucket of colorful flowers
- A selection of offerings made from lettuce, seafood, watermelon, molasses, plantains, white wine, and coffee
- Ocean water; if you don't have this available, putting salt in water can be a good alternative

There are ready-made kits containing everything you need for setting up a shrine for Yemaya, but you're advised to also use your creativity. If you have godparents (*through the religion*), they can also help you figure out what you need. For example, which image you use will depend on what's traditionally used in the religion you follow. In Yoruba, she is depicted as an Orisha. In Santeria, her most common image is *La Virgen de Regla*, but she can also be portrayed as the Sea Goddess.

After gathering your ingredients, you can start setting up the shrine:

1. Begin by draping the blue cloth over the surface of the base.
2. Place the image of the goddess in the center and scatter the shells, silver objects, pearls, fans, and the small items that symbolize Yemaya.
3. Place the sopera with the offerings and the bowl with the water in front of the main symbol.
4. Put one of the candles on the left side of the symbol and the other on the right.
5. Scatter the flowers between the other items.
6. Fold the dress (or leave it unfolded, depending on your space) and leave it on the far left side with the crown on top.
7. Place the incense on the left. Light it only before your practice, along with the candles.

How to Give Offerings and Clear Them

Before using the shrine, don't forget to bless it by dedicating a short prayer to the goddess. After this, you can start presenting the offerings. Be generous, and leave something every day. Say a prayer or do a quick meditation every time you do. If you're leaving food items, ensure they won't stay more than two or three days. Live flowers will also wilt, so you'll need to replace them. Non-perishable items can remain for as long as you need them or until you decide to replace them with other objects. Replace any burned-out candles as soon as possible.

Apart from the items listed above, you can also leave items that reflect personal needs and wants. If you play an instrument or sing, you can also use these talents to honor the Orisha. You can even leave small instruments in the sacred space. The number of the small items (like the silver objects, pearls, or shells) should be seven, as this is the number of seas she governs. If you feel that your space is getting too crowded, remove some items. You can always start adding new objects as you continue your daily veneration of the goddess.

You can also leave offerings when you seek Yemaya's wisdom, need a maternal figure, or a helping hand for healing from emotional trauma. Be polite when you make an offering at the shrine, and never leave an offering while asking for something harmful. Remember, she has a vengeful side too, and you don't want to anger her.

Additional Tips for Setting and Caring for Your Shrine

There are very few rules on how you can or cannot build a shrine for Yemaya. She is the goddess of many faces, and as long as you include some of the traditional elements associated with any of her traits, you can go on to personalize your space as you like. For newbies, it's generally recommended to have only a small shrine in your home. This will allow you to concentrate your power. It will also make it easier to nurture it with positive energy and take care of it in general. You'll need to keep it clean – physically and spiritually. The easiest way to do both is to cover it with a large piece of blue cloth when you aren't using it or have visitors who aren't familiar with your religion.

Occasionally you can remove everything, clean the dust and other debris, and put everything back onto your shrine. Make sure you cleanse it regularly with incense to ward off negative energies, as these can hinder your communication with the goddess. Not leaving perishable items on for too long is another way to keep negative energies away. Pay attention to Yemaya's clues, too, regarding the shrine and the offerings. Sometimes, she will tell you what to prepare next. Listen to her advice even if it sounds strange to you. She only wishes for you to find the balance you need.

Chapter 8: Spiritual Baths and Spells

As the mother of all Orishas and the patron of waters, Yemaya can help with various issues related to femininity and spiritual healing. Now that you've learned her correspondences, you can delve into using them to harness the goddess's essence. This chapter offers recipes for ritual baths and spells for self-love, fertility, and healing emotional wounds or trauma.

Ritual baths can be therapeutic and healing.
https://unsplash.com/photos/5PVLPi7oenA

Healing Bath from Yemaya's Hand

Taking a healing bath is a great way to use Yemaya's power for spiritual healing. This one will help you attract positive energy and spiritual prosperity, flush out negative energy, and ward it off in the future. You can take this easy-to-prepare bath at any time of the day.

You will need the following:

- 1 coconut soap only you use
- Sea water or regular water with sea salt added to it (as needed)
- Lavender perfume only you use
- Cane molasses
- A large blue candle (it has to be tall enough so the water doesn't cover its tip)
- A tall container
- Coconut water
- Blue or Indigo wash

Instructions:

1. Add the Indigo or Blue wash, lavender perfume, cane molasses, and coconut water to the container.
2. Pour in ¾ of the water and stir in a clockwise direction with your hands. While doing this, silently ask the goddess for prosperity, health, balance, abundance, peace, or anything you want.
3. Put the candle in the middle of the container and add more water if there is enough space, but be careful not to cover the candle.
4. Light the candle and gaze into its flame. Feel how the warmth radiates from it, filling you with love and care.
5. Ask Yemaya to empower the light to have an even more powerful effect when lighting your heart up.
6. When you feel ready, snuff out the candle. If there is any wax in the water, strain it.
7. Fill your bath with warm water by adjusting the temperature to your liking.
8. Place the container with the water blessed by Yemaya on the bathtub's edge.

9. Enter into the water and wash with coconut soap. It will purify your body from negative energies, and the scent of the soap will also attract positive energy.
10. Take the container and slowly pour the water over your body, starting from your neck and going downwards.
11. Reinforce your request for prosperity, health, balance, abundance, peace, or anything else you want.
12. If possible, allow the water to dry naturally and feel positivity coursing through your body. If you're cold, pat dry with a towel.
13. Don't forget to clean the bathtub after you're done to remove the negativity from your vicinity.
14. Take this bath every week (preferably on a Saturday), and you'll receive many blessings from Yemaya. The success you've asked for will soon begin.

Full Moon Bath Ritual

With the full moon bath ritual, you can call on the deepest power of the supreme mother goddess. It will help you heal through spiritual growth, self-love, and self-acceptance. You will need to take it at night when the moon is in the highest position.

You will need the following:
- 7 blue candles
- 7 white rose petals
- 1 moonstone or other lunar stone
- 7 pinches of sea salt
- 7 drops of peppermint, passionflower, or lavender essential oil

Instructions:
1. Start drawing a bath. While the tub is filling, place the candles around its edge and light them.
2. Gazing into the candlelight, take a few breaths and focus on the issue that needs to be eliminated from your mind so you can heal.
3. Add salt and essential oils to the bathwater. As you do, call on Yemaya and ask her to fill your heart.

4. Take a deep breath and enter the tub. As you immerse yourself in the water, feel the caring touch of the goddess, healing you.
5. Take as much time as you need soaking, and let her heal your deepest wounds.
6. Step out of the tub and pat yourself dry with a towel when you're ready.
7. Before you drain the water, place the rose petals on the edge of the tub as an offering to Yemaya while saying the following:

"Yemaya, our mother and the goddess of the water.

Come to this place and be with me.

Goddess of the rivers, lakes, and oceans,

Your beauty brings the flow of power.

I ask you to heal my soul, mind, and body.

With the help of your love, I will become whole again.

Ashe, great goddess."

Yemaya's Spell for Love

If you live near a large body of water (ocean, sea, lake, river, etc.), enacting Yemaya's love spell will be the perfect way to attract or deepen romantic feelings. And even if you don't, you can still perform a modified version of the spell. With the help of this spell, anyone can evoke Yemaya's power and attract love into their lives. It is particularly effective when enacted on a Saturday, Yemaya's sacred day. However, it only works if there is already attraction between you and the desired person.

You will need the following:
- 1 blue candle
- 1 melon
- Cane molasses
- Vanilla extract
- Brown sugar
- 2 blue ribbons
- Paper and a red pen

Instructions:
1. Place everything on your altar or shrine, and settle in front of it.
2. Light the candle and call on Yemaya.
3. Write down your name, the name of your love, and the date of birth for both of you seven times.
4. Turn the paper, and write what you need help with on the other side. For example, if you're already in a relationship, you can ask the goddess to strengthen your love for each other. If you aren't in a relationship with the person, you can ask the goddess to help either of you make the first step.
5. Cut off the top of the melon, and insert the paper into it.
6. Pour the sugar, vanilla extract, and cane molasses into the melon. Ask Yemaya to sweeten your heart as you're doing it with the melon.
7. Place the top of the melon back from where you cut it, and secure it into place by tying the ribbons around the melon. You can use a piece of tape to make it more secure.
8. Put the melon beside the candle, and keep it here until the candle burns down completely.
9. If you live by the water, carry the melon to the water and offer it to Yemaya. Place seven coins beside it and leave it there.
10. If you don't live near water, place the melon in your garden or outside your window. Leave it there for the goddess for a few days.
11. Walk away without looking back.
12. When you get home, give heartfelt thanks to the goddess by offering a prayer of gratitude.
13. Soon, the goddess will grant your request, and the love in your heart and the heart of your loved one will deepen.

New Moon Ritual

The goddess's power can also be harnessed around the new moon. During this period, you can ask her for new opportunities, fertility, or to help you move on from a traumatic experience and start a new chapter in your life.

You will need the following:
- The symbol of Yemaya
- 7 coins
- 1 blue candle
- Any offerings you want to give to Yemaya

Instructions:
1. Start by lighting the candle on the day of the new moon. The candle should be placed next to the symbol and any other offerings you want to make.
2. Hold a coin in your hands and call on Yemaya. Ask her for whatever you need for the new moon to bring.
3. Gaze into the candle flame and focus on your inquiry.
4. When you're ready, offer a prayer of gratitude to the goddess and put the coin down next to the other offerings before extinguishing the candle.
5. Repeat this for seven consecutive days, leaving a coin each time.
6. At the end of the seventh day, look at all the coins you've left for the goddess. Use them as a reminder of what inspired you to reach out to Yemaya.
7. The goddess will soon grant your wishes. When she does, you can remove the coins from the altar while expressing your gratitude once more.

Yemaya's Self-Confidence Ritual

This is another seven-day ritual dedicated to the mother goddess, except this one can be done at any time of the month. It invokes Yemaya's power with the help of seven candles and fills you with self-confidence and love.

You will need the following:
- 7 blue or white candles (pick whichever color resonates with you the most)
- 1 container

Instructions:
1. Place all the colors on the altar or shrine, and settle in front of it.
2. At nightfall, light one candle and call on Yemaya.
3. Focus your gaze on the flame, and envision how its warmth envelops you.
4. Visualize Yemaya's energy accompanying the warmth by forming a glowing orb around you.
5. Ask Yemaya to help you gain confidence in your ability to persevere and become the person you wish to be.
6. Let the candle burn out and leave it at the altar.
7. Repeat this for six more days.
8. On the seventh night, collect all the wax from the candles into a container.
9. Place the container on your windowsill to charge the wax with moonlight, which contains the goddess's essence.
10. You will soon start gaining confidence. Make sure you thank the goddess for her blessings.

Renewal Bath

This bath will help you recharge and fill your body and spirit with new, positive energy with the help of Yemaya. It only has a few simple ingredients and can be done any time of the week or month.

You will need the following:
- White flower petals
- 4 cups of water
- 1 teaspoon of cinnamon
- Dried raspberries or a splash of raspberry vinaigrette (if you're allergic to berries, omit this ingredient)
- 1 white candle

Instructions:
1. Pour the water into a pot and bring it to a boil.
2. Add the cinnamon, flower petals, and raspberries/vinaigrette into the boiling water.

3. Turn off the heat and let the water infuse with the rest of the ingredients for 15 minutes.
4. In the meantime, prepare a bath and light a candle you've placed on the edge of the tub.
5. Add the infused water to your bathwater, and mix it with your hand.
6. Immerse yourself in the water while calling on Yemaya.
7. Start focusing on what you need more energy for and tell this to the goddess.
8. Let her remove all the negativity from your body, mind, and soul and replace it with positivity.
9. As you relax and begin to feel renewed, say thanks to the goddess.
10. Leave the tub, snuff out the candle, and let yourself air dry.
11. You can follow up with your favorite beauty ritual, such as applying lotions, oils, serums, etc.

Spell for Recharging through Yemaya

This spell also works for recharging your energies with the help of the mother goddess. It allows you to form a deeper bond with Yemaya and tie yourself to her spiritually, which will go a long way for any healing or spiritual growth you need help with in the future.

You will need the following:

- 1 bowl of water
- A few drops of your favorite essential oil
- 1 symbol of Yemaya
- 1 blue candle

Instructions:

1. Place everything on your altar or shrine and prepare yourself for the ritual by taking a few deep breaths.
2. Add the essential oil to the water and light the candle.
3. Look at the symbol of the goddess and place one of your hands over it.
4. Place your other hand over the water. Visualize an energy channel being opened to receive positive energy.

5. Ask the goddess to bless you with positivity and help you chase away the negative influences by saying:

   "Mother Goddess, I ask you now for the renewal of my soul. Please send me your blessings and help me remain active and healthy."

6. Envision the positive energy traveling from the image of the goddess into the water.
7. When you feel you've channeled enough positivity into the water, immerse your hands in it.
8. Let your hand soak for half a minute, then pat it dry.
9. Repeat as often as you need to recharge yourself.

Yemaya's Self-Love Jar

With the help of a few items associated with Yemaya's power, you can create a jar full of positivity that will remind you of your best qualities. Anytime you feel a lack of self-love, you'll just have to look at the jar, and the goddess will remind you that you are worthy of love and compassion.

You will need the following:

- 1 large jar with a lid
- Sea salt
- Cane molasses
- Cinnamon
- Dried white flower petals
- 7 coins
- Small shells
- 1 blue candle
- 1 symbol of the goddess
- Dried seaweed
- Small figures of water creatures
- Paper and pen

Instructions:

1. Place everything on your altar in front of the divine symbol and light the candle.

2. Start putting everything into the jar. With each item, take a small break and say something positive about yourself.
3. On the paper, write what you're asking for from the goddess. For example, you can ask her to remind you of your self-worth, help you gain more confidence, or cultivate deeper self-love.
4. Place the paper into the jar and say a silent prayer to the goddess.
5. Close the jar, take the candle, and allow the wax to drip down around the lid while turning the jar.
6. As the wax hardens and forms a seal, say thanks for the goddess's blessing that you'll receive.

Fertility Ritual

This traditional Yoruba ritual has been used by young women who want to conceive a child. Apart from this, Yemaya can grant you fertility in many other aspects of life, such as art, work, and even cultivating relationships. The colors and seeds of the pumpkin symbolize her power over nature and fertility.

You will need the following:
- 1 pumpkin
- 1 blue candle
- 1 pencil
- 1 brown paper bag
- A representation of the Yemaya

Instructions:
1. Place the blue candle in front of the representation of Yemaya on your altar or shrine and light it.
2. Close your eyes and focus on manifesting your wishes. Saying them out loud often helps.
3. Open your eyes and carve a round opening in the pumpkin.
4. Take the pencil and write your wishes down on a piece of the paper bag.
5. Place the piece of paper inside the pumpkin, then pour candle wax on top of it.
6. After ensuring the pumpkin has been sealed with the wax, place it over your stomach, repeating your wishes.

7. When you feel your wishes have been heard, take the pumpkin to the nearest water source, and offer it to Yemaya. Alternatively, you can leave it on your windowsill so it can charge through the moon.

You may leave the candle burning for a short period after the ritual is completed. However, if you are going to leave it unattended, it's best to snuff it out. You can relight the candle any time you want to during the next seven days.

Yemaya's Healing Elixir

Not only is this simple elixir beneficial for your health, but you can also charge it with Yemaya's power. Prepare it on the night of the full moon, and you'll receive the benefits the next day.

You will need the following:
- Water - as needed (you can prepare several cups of the elixir and consume them one by one throughout the day)
- Cinnamon sticks
- 1 kettle
- 1 marker
- 1 glass jar

Instructions:
1. Draw a shell at the bottom of the jar to symbolize Yemaya. While doing this, focus on calling on her.
2. Fill the jar with as many cups of water as you want and ask for Yemaya's blessing.
3. Place the jar on the windowsill where it can bask in the moonlight and leave it overnight.
4. In the morning, pour the water from the jar into a kettle, bring it to a boil, and pour it back into the jar.
5. Place the cinnamon sticks into the water and visualize them releasing the positive energy Yemaya poured into them during the night.
6. Let the cinnamon infuse the water for 10 minutes, and your elixir will be ready to drink.

7. As you drink it, imagine Yemaya's love spreading through your body and healing you.

Disclaimer

The transfer of Yemaya's essence can have an incredibly powerful effect on the recipient of this nurturing energy. Using the goddess's power, you can balance out your spiritual energy, allowing you to become re-energized and helping you face life's challenges more easily. That being said, Yemaya's power can't cure any mental illness. If you suspect that you have any psychological condition, you should consult a relevant healthcare specialist regarding treatment. Once your doctor has established a diagnosis and conventional treatment plan, you can revisit the possibility of reaching out to the goddess to empower yourself through the healing process.

If you've already been diagnosed with a mental illness, wait until you feel strong enough to do any ritual evoking Yemaya. Receiving her healing energy can be an overwhelming experience, even for healthy minds. For beginners, her messages can be confusing, and her energy can be too powerful. If your mental well-being is not at its best, receiving spiritual messages can do more harm than good. Even if you can receive her messages, not being in the best mind frame can affect your ability to honor the goddess appropriately.

Chapter 9: Sacred Days and Festivals

Festivals and rituals are common ways to pay tribute to our beloved Orisha deities and have been taking place for years. Festivals honoring Yemaya are especially popular because of her prominence among the other orishas. After all, she is called the mother of all for a reason. Throughout history, the sea and ocean have remained sacred places for West Africans due to the many legends associated with them. There are several powerful female figures among the Orisha deities, among whom Yemaya is notable. She symbolizes a maternal relationship because of her association with water and fertility.

Furthermore, the ocean played a significant role in the forced crossings of the slave trade. Enslaved people who survived the journey set the custom of making offerings to the goddess and passed these practices down to their descendants. Thus originated the festivals celebrating the glorious Orisha of the oceans and sea, Yemaya.

Festivals and rituals are a wonderful way to pay tribute to the Orishas.
https://unsplash.com/photos/-p7amImLLqs

While one major Lemanja festival takes place on February 2nd in several places around the world, other smaller celebrations also occur throughout the year. The main celebration is held in Salvador and Sao Paulo and includes a variety of activities like dancing, singing, praying, feasting, and engaging in other rituals. During these festivals, it is customary to invoke Yemaya and ask for her blessings, using the themes and ritual tools covered in earlier chapters. This chapter will be a guide to understanding the various festivities associated with the goddess Yemaya and how you can participate in them.

Festival of Iemanjá in Salvador

Considered one of the most popular celebrations in Salvador, Bahia, the Iemanjá festival pays homage to the ocean goddess Yemaya and has been taking place since contemporary times. Over the years, it has retained its popularity and strength and is still one of the most essential manifestations of the city. The event, which is held on February 2, is filled with the fervor and zeal of the goddess's ardent devotees. It is not only filled with old traditions and practices but is also intense in the sense that numerous people partake in the activities with complete fervor. This festival is therefore regarded as an integral part of Salvador's heritage. It is safeguarded by the national registry to protect Afro-Brazilian cultures and other religious manifestations.

The biggest celebration usually takes place in the neighborhood of Rio Vermelho, located in the Fishermen's Colony. The place is decorated with charms and theme colors and is visited by people from all over the world who want to deliver gifts to Yemaya. Nowadays, most people only place flowers in the sea because other charms and offerings like mirrors, soaps, jewelry, or perfumes can cause damage to marine life. These are the guidelines you should follow if you're planning to attend the Yemaya festivities in Salvador, Brazil:

- The festivities of the Iemanjá celebration begin a day before the actual festival, on the night of February 1st. So, it's a good idea to arrive early at Casa de Iemanjá to fully explore the cultural heritage associated with the festival. People start by watching the sun rise while enjoying the sand between their toes and listening to the traditional Candomble and Umbanda drums playing in the background.

- The festivities officially begin at dawn with beautiful fireworks adorning the sky. People can leave offerings from early in the day to late at night.

- The celebration procession carries the offerings in boats to deliver them to Yemaya. This takes place at about 4 p.m. when the fishermen go out to sea. To join the procession, you should get there early and find a seat on one of the boats. You can hire a boat at any other time too, but leaving the procession with flower baskets will be a special experience.

- While there are no limitations to what you want to wear, it's best to wear something blue or white to show respect. This will portray your willingness to learn about the Yoruba culture, even if you're not one of the initiated.

- There are various recreational groups passing along the waterfront throughout the day, including capoeira, samba, and percussion groups. There are also many parties and shows filled with dancing, singing, and chanting in many places near the festival.

The Iemanjá Festival in Other Parts of the City

Salvador is a hub of celebrations in the name of Yemaya. She is a more beloved Orisha than any other female goddess and has an air of importance about her. Celebrations in other parts of the city include the Solar de Unhao, which happens during the last week of January. People only present flower offerings to the goddess during this event and ask for her guidance.

Another festival happens in Itapua right before the Yemanja festival. It is known as Lavagem de Itapua and takes place on February 13th. During this celebration, the followers of Yemaya walk the streets dressed according to the theme for the occasion. They carry pots with flowers and fragrant water to cleanse the church's staircase. Many cultural groups roam the streets celebrating the Queen of the Sea and pay tribute to her legacy by offering various charms, singing songs, and dancing.

Yemoja Festival in Ibadan, Nigeria

Another prominent region where the goddess Yemaya is celebrated is in Nigeria, particularly Ibadan, New Oyo. Every year, Yoruba followers in Nigeria gather together and offer their thanks to the Goddess and Queen of the Sea, along with celebrating other Yoruba gods. They believe this is an essential practice in order to pay homage to their ancestral beliefs and traditional roots.

During this annual festival, the people start the day with a traditional dance, music, and some prayers invoking Yemaya. As Yemoja is considered the mother of all Orisha, she has more importance than any other Orisha. This prominent festival gains public attention based on the fact that it lasts 17 whole days and is said to be as old as the Yoruba culture. The celebration starts in October and ends on the last day of the month. The grand finale, which happens on October 31st, includes traditional dances in front of the temple of Yemoja.

Yemaya devotees perfect their dances before the celebration in order to correctly match the rhythm of the music. Inside the temple, there is a statue of Yemoja breastfeeding a baby. The dedicated followers of Yemaya sing songs, pray, chant, and give thanks to the mother goddess for her blessings. They thank the Orisha for keeping them healthy and prosperous during the past year and pray for her blessings for the coming year. Then, they move to the river to make their offerings.

Inside the temple of Yemoja, the chief of the village prepares the various offerings needed to be presented to the river goddess. In front of him is the statue of Ogunleki, next to which some hollowed-out calabashes are placed. Calabashes have a prominent role in Yoruba history and are thus considered sacred fruit. The chief drops the offerings into the calabashes while speaking sacred words of prayer to the mother goddess Yemoja.

Once these offerings have been prepared, the chief priest associated with Yemoja says a few prayers with his hands outstretched. The devotees respond to this prayer with *ase* (the traditional ending to prayer in Yoruba culture) and begin the procession. The procession starts from the temple and goes all the way to the river to present the offerings to Yemaya. The women are dressed in complete white and carry the food offerings in calabashes. Each calabash carries different food offerings, including cooked beans and rice, fruits, porridge, and other associated food items for Yemoja. The other participants follow the calabash carriers all the way to the river.

The river is considered to be inhabited by guiding spirits connected with Yemoja. Everyone makes pledges with the spirits, and during the next festival, they redeem their pledges by making different offerings to the spirits. This expression of gratitude helps the devotees plan and pray for the future as well. When the pledges and prayers at the river are completed, the chief priestess gathers some of the water from the river and sprinkles it on her fellow calabash carriers and Yemoja devotees. Some of this water is also collected and used for medicinal purposes and ritual baths.

The women play an integral part in the festivals of Yemoja – from carrying the calabashes to preparing the offerings and performing priestess duties; the female population has imperative roles in the sacred celebration. The processional celebration takes place over the next few days, along with a number of other traditional activities.

On the last day of the festival, the new initiates have to cut their hair and wear unique beads designed for new members. The jewelry is composed of blue and red beads that form a choker-like necklace. After a while, the new members are finally permitted to wear the long, white bead necklaces worn by other devotees. The procession concludes with the presentation of food offerings at the river's edge. Each item is put into the river one at a time and is taken away by the current.

Iemanjá Celebrations in Uruguay

Iemanjá celebrations also take place annually in Uruguay on February 2 and are considered to be one of the most festive occasions in the country. During this festival, many tourists are attracted to Ramirez Beach. While festivities begin right after sunrise, noticeable crowds start to gather in the afternoon to enjoy the traditional music associated with Uruguayan people and Yoruba history. This involves rapid drumming sounds along with some fast music. Many street vendors line the edge of the beach, selling charms, necklaces, candles, posters, clothes, and food items relevant to Yemaya.

In the evening, the devotees start to prepare their altars dedicated to Yemaya. These structures are usually made with sand from the beach. People place all kinds of offerings to the goddess on this altar, along with a statue. The statue is surrounded by blue and white candles, which are lit after dusk. Some people also place handcrafted food or prepare food items that the goddess favors. After preparing the altar, the devotees sit down and look at the beautiful sunset from the beach while praying to the goddess. After sundown, the festivities increase. Uruguayan music spreads across the beach and lasts all night. The offerings are floated across the sea until they're swept away by the current.

Many people also take part in festive dances and whirling after nightfall. This is when the festival is at its peak. The participants in the dance often fall into a spiritual trance when whirling around frenetically. The devotees and any other participants dress in long, white, flowing skirts or dresses. They can be seen bowing to the queen of the sea and staying prostrate on the ground. Then, they walk slowly into the sea until the water comes up to their knees. Here, they present their offerings to Yemaya, say a few prayers, and walk back to shore without turning their backs as a sign of respect. Although there aren't many properly initiated worshippers of Yemaya, the festival usually attracts a large crowd of people who come to participate in the traditions. Most of them are just there to observe from the sidelines, while some take part in the activities and leave offerings for the goddess.

Yemaya Festival in Fernihurst, VIC

As you already know, the Yemaya festival has gained popularity all over the globe. Yoruba festivals and traditions aren't just practiced in native regions anymore but in various places all around the world. One of these major Yemaya festivals is celebrated at Fernihurst, Victoria, near Melbourne, Australia. The vibrant, multi-day event is a sight to see and is considered to be the experience of a lifetime. The festival is initiated with some prayers to the goddess, followed by an honorary celebration paying tribute to the traditional owners of the region. People pray to the goddess for blessings and cleansing of their spirits and hope to have the upcoming days full of familial and positive energy.

The devoted community celebrating this festival makes it possible for the event to be full of artistic possibilities and creative spirit. Celebrated along the Loddon River, the participants are given an open landscape to explore the water and nearby regions for self-exploration. As soon as you get there, you'll be immersed in a colorful world filled with music, dance, and celebratory spirit. The decor is unique and mesmerizing, complete with psychedelic patterns, warm lighting, abstract designs, and beautiful hanging charms.

This festival is unlike any other traditional Yemoja festival and consists of modern performances on the main stage. The unique aspect of this event is the incorporation of a modern twist into the traditional practices which are used to celebrate the goddess Yemaya. The pulsing rhythms make everyone move along with the music, which creates an almost trance-like state at the gathering. Devotees and guests are encouraged to move freely and become at one with the music. A special, fluid-like dance is commonly observed during these performances. Most of these musical performances symbolize personal transformation and help deepen your connection with the goddess, Yemaya. During the day, upbeat pop music plays across the speakers, whereas trance-like, mind-bending music takes over the festival once the sun sets.

If you're a part of the festival to self-explore and connect yourself with the goddess, it will hardly benefit you if you're a fly on the wall. Although there's nothing against observing the festivities, it will do you some good to actually participate in the dances and other practices to feel a part of the culture. The locals and festival organizers encourage the participants to take part in the visual and performing arts. The festival's open space gives participants the advantage of adding a spark to the music. Guests even have the option of creating their own music by jamming with anyone looking to work an instrument.

The guests can further feed their creative impulses by working with arts and crafts supplies to create unique treasures that can be later presented as offerings to the goddess or used to decorate her altar. This Yemaya festival can prove to be a wonderful bonding experience encouraging collaborative effort, peace, harmony, and unconditional love. Even if you're somewhat of a wallflower, try to throw yourself into the mix of this festival to enjoy the full experience. Treat everyone like a big family, and you'll be surprised to see how you're welcomed with open arms.

Yemaya Festivities in Pelotas

Another birthplace for traditional festivals celebrating the sea goddess, Yemaya, is Pelatos, Rio Grande. It is customary for the picture of Nossa Senhora to be carried across the city to the port of Pelatos on February 2nd. The boat brings aboard Yoruba practitioners who carry the image of Yemoja before the end of the Catholic feast, which is watched by thousands of people.

Festa da Conceição da Praia

One of the oldest religious festivals taking place in Brazil, the *Festa da Conceiço da Praia*, pays homage to the glorious patroness of Bahia. The theme of the party relates to the Immaculate Conception, which refers to a theme of the church but is also often related to the mother goddess, Yemoja. With the basilica's choir singing in the background, a procession of priests, seminarians, and other people march across the city, paying tribute to Nossa Senhora da Conceicao.

Preparations for the festival start at 5 in the morning, but the main celebrations start after 9 a.m. If you want to get a good view of the procession, it's best to arrive early. The musical performances are incredible and include many traditional aspects. The procession leaves Conceicao da Praia at 10:30 a.m. and returns after about 12 hours. After that, a huge celebration ensues, which includes baskets of offerings to the goddess, food stalls, and many other activities.

Other Yemaya Festivals in Sao Paulo

Sao Paulo also hosts a few Iemanjá festivals and feasts to pay tribute to the goddess of the sea. These usually take place during the first two weeks of December. During these festivals, many cars are decorated with Yoruba charms and colors. For Yemaya, the colors blue and white are most prominent in every decoration. Some of these cars travel hundreds of miles from the Sao Paulo Mountains to the beach. On the Praia Grande beach, numerous people gather near the statue of Yemoja.

New Year's Celebrations in Brazil

Many people also pray to Yemoja at the beginning of the New Year to ask for her blessings for the coming year. Rio de Janeiro, in particular, sees millions of devotees dressed in religious attire which matches the color themes of Yemaya. These people usually gather on the Copacabana beach to watch fireworks and make offerings to the goddess. These offerings can include flowers, food items, fruits, charms, etc. Some people send their offerings to Yemoja in small, wooden toy boats. Many shops sell beautiful paintings of the goddess, depicting her rising from the sea as a mermaid. Leaving floating candles along the coast is also a pretty common practice during this time.

Yemaya, the glorious goddess of the rivers, sea, and fertility, is celebrated all around the world. There are countless devotees who make meaningful offerings every year at these festivals. Whether it's the annual Iemanjá festival in Salvador, Bahia, or the Iemanjá festival in Ibadan, both locals, and foreigners celebrate these occasions with full zest. The more modern festivals are also carried out with great zeal, albeit a bit differently than the traditional events. The practices carried out during these festivals help many people get more familiar with their roots, connect with their spirituality, and honor the Orisha goddess Yemaya. No matter what stage of your spiritual journey you're at, celebrating Yemaya with your best intentions will get you one step closer to making a true connection with the Mother Goddess.

Chapter 10: Daily Rituals to Honor Yemaya

There are a number of different rituals and practices you can incorporate into your daily life if you're looking to honor Yemaya.

As Yemaya is the Orisha of the sea, many of these rituals involve water or items associated with water. Additionally, as the Orisha of motherhood, many of the rituals to honor her are fertility rituals.

In this last chapter, we'll look at ways you can honor Yemaya in your everyday life, helping you to create a long and lasting relationship with her. Some of these rituals include making offerings to the sea, creating an altar for Yemaya, taking a spiritual bath, conducting a healing ritual, and more.

Making Offerings to the Sea

If you live near the sea or plan on visiting the seaside, one of the most effective daily rituals to Yemaya is to make your offerings directly to the sea. These offerings can take the shape of a range of items, including:

- Fish
- Fruit
- Candles
- Flowers
- Honey

- Mirrors
- Foods
- Statues of Yemaya

If you plan on immersing your offerings in the sea, make sure that they are biodegradable and will do no damage to the waters they will be immersed in. For example, if you're going to immerse an idol, make sure that it and any paint on it are eco-friendly. The last thing you want is to unwittingly do further damage to the oceans while trying to honor Yemaya.

Another way to make offerings directly to the sea is to make a small vessel out of paper or paper mache. You can decorate the vessel with symbols of Yemaya, fill it with small offerings, and allow the boat to float away on the water.

Once you have made your offering, light a candle and set it in the sand. Then send out a prayer to Yemaya, offering your gratitude for the good luck and blessings that she has brought into your life.

After offering your prayer, make sure you extinguish the candle and take it home with you so that it does not accidentally injure another visitor at the beach.

Create an Altar and Make Your Offerings

If you don't live near the sea (or are unable to visit frequently), there's no reason to worry. You can also build an altar to Yemaya in your own home and make your offerings at the altar.

The altar you build should be populated with representations of Yemaya. This can include an image of her, cowrie shells and other types of shells, a sopera, blue cloth, and more.

Once you have constructed and are satisfied with your altar to Yemaya, the next step is to make your offerings. When you make your offerings at the altar, make sure to light a candle and offer a prayer to the Orisha. After you finish your prayer, you can either extinguish the candle or leave it to burn off on its own.

Conduct a Cowrie Ritual

Cowrie shells are intrinsically linked to Yemaya, and most altars to the Orisha hold at least a few of these shells. If you have access to cowrie shells, you can use them to conduct a ritual to Yemaya.

Tiger Cowrie Ritual

You will need the following:

- 1 tiger cowrie shell
- Frankincense oil

This ritual should be conducted when you're ready to start a new project. It is a way of honoring Yemaya as the Orisha of motherhood while also calling on her to bless your new undertaking.

To conduct the ritual, you should insert something representative of your project into the belly of the tiger cowrie shell. Some ideas include:

- A piece of paper on which you have written your goals for the project.
- A crystal chip to represent the energy you want to imbue your project with.
- A small item that is representative of the project – for example, if you're starting a new sewing project, you may place a scrap of fabric inside the shell.

Once you place the item in the belly of the shell, you should rub the entrance with the frankincense oil. This protects the energy you have imbued the shell with. After rubbing the oil into the shell, say a prayer to Yemaya, asking for good luck in your project.

On the night of the new moon, place the shell with the item in it on a windowsill. The new moon is the ideal time to begin your new project, and the cowrie shell with your chosen item inside it represents creativity. The shell is "pregnant" with a seed, and the new moon is the perfect time to allow it to grow.

Small Cowrie Ritual

Small cowries are the ones that are usually bought in bulk. These are generally easy to source, making this ritual one that anyone can perform.

You will need the following:

- 2 containers of the same size
- Enough small cowrie shells to fill one container

To perform this ritual, you should first fill one container to the brim with cowries. Then, each day, take out one cowrie. Facing the east, hold it so that the mouth of the shell is facing you.

Keeping Yemaya and your devotion to her in your mind, speak out loud to the shell. What you tell the shell differs from person to person – it may be an articulation of your dreams, values, hopes, or anything else. The shell essentially serves as a connection to Yemaya, and speaking to the cowrie is a way of speaking to Yemaya.

Once you have finished speaking and filled the shell with your voice, place it in the second container. Repeat this ritual daily.

When you have run out of cowries, cleanse the filled cowries using fresh water, and allow them to dry. The water will carry your words to Yemaya, and you can reuse the cowries to continue this ritual.

Conduct a Venus Comb Murex Ritual

Aside from cowrie shells, you can use any other shell to connect with Yemaya. The Venus Comb Murex is a popular option because of the association of the shell with combs (as its name indicates), grooming, beauty, and women. This ritual is a way of honoring aspects of yourself that often aren't recognized or appreciated the way they should be.

You will need the following:
- 1 shell of any kind
- 1 Venus Comb Murex. If you cannot source a physical shell, an image of one will do
- 1 bottle or pitcher of water
- 1 blue bowl
- 1 container of salt
- Blue and white beads – 7 or more
- 12 inches of string
- Glue
- 1 hair comb
- 2 glasses of drinking water
- Goldfish crackers

- Music associated with Yemaya – this can be ocean sounds or devotional music created to honor her

For this ritual, you should wear blue and white and follow the steps below:

1. Place the shell in front of the bowl.
2. Position yourself comfortably – you can also do this ritual sitting down if you prefer.
3. Take three deep breaths.
4. Gently pour the water into the bowl.
5. Once you have poured the water into the bowl, add salt into the water one pinch at a time.
6. Pick up one bead. Hold it in your hands and imbue it with a part of yourself that you feel isn't recognized or appreciated. You can do this by making a statement out loud. For example, you might say, *"I'm good at working in a team."* Once you imbue the bead with your energy, place it in the water.
7. Repeat the above step for each bead.
8. Once you've placed all the beads in the water, swirl the water clockwise with your fingers, allowing energy to build in the bowl, water, and beads. As you do this, imagine your words being transmitted to Yemaya.
9. One at a time, pull the beads from the water and string them on your thread. Tie a knot, and reinforce it with a drop of glue once the beads and thread have dried.
10. Look at the (picture of the) Venus Comb Murex and comb your hair, imagining Yemaya helping you while you do so. This act of self-care is a way to build up your self-esteem.
11. Once the bracelet and glue have dried, slip it onto your hand. Your bracelet, now imbued with Yemaya's power, is a reminder that while you cannot control how other people think and act, you can control how you think about yourself and present yourself to the world.
12. Play music and dance, allowing your energy to fill the room. Afterward, ground yourself by consuming a few goldfish crackers.
13. Take a drink from one glass of water, blessing your ritual and praying to Yemaya while you do so.

14. Finish by making an offering to Yemaya. You can do this by incorporating the other glass of water into your altar, or you can simply put it into the earth (the soil from a potted plant will work). Alternatively, you can take a shower and pour the glass of water on yourself as part of your shower.

Take Part in a Bath Ritual

Bath rituals are a powerful way to connect with and honor Yemaya, given how intrinsically connected they are to water. You can conduct bath rituals in your own bathroom or in a body of water.

Home Bath Ritual

You will need the following:
- A bathtub
- An altar to Yemaya
- ¼ cup of sea salt
- 7 drops of eucalyptus oil

Instructions:
1. First, create an altar for Yemaya in your bathroom. You can do this by bringing in a small side table and covering it with a blue cloth. Then, fill the altar with an image of Yemaya and ocean-related objects, such as seashells, pearls (real if possible), ocean-inspired art, and so on. You can also add some blue and white flowers to the altar.
2. Next, fill your bathtub with warm water.
3. Add the sea salt and eucalyptus oil to the water, gently mixing to incorporate them fully.
4. While praying to Yemaya, immerse yourself in the water. You can pray out loud or silently - Yemaya will hear you either way. This prayer can take the form of anything you wish - you can take the opportunity to speak with Yemaya about your fears and worries, vocalize your regrets, or thank her for your blessings. Next, ask her to remove any blocks that are preventing you from reaching your true potential and moving forward in life. Conclude your prayer by thanking her for her love and compassion.

5. When you have finished praying, remove the drain plug and allow the water in the bathtub to drain away. As the water drains, it will take all the negativity you released in your prayer along with it.

Sea/Ocean/River Bath Ritual

If you live near an accessible body of water, you can try this ritual. For this bath ritual, you will need the following:

- Cane molasses
- Offerings to Yemaya – a good option is an offering of blue and white flowers. Make sure that the offerings you choose are eco-friendly and can be immersed in a body of water without causing damage to the ecosystem.

Instructions:

1. Walk into the water and allow the water to rinse the molasses away from your body. As the water washes away the molasses, think of yourself being cleansed and purified by the power of Yemaya.
2. As the water is washing away the molasses, release your offerings into the water and thank Yemaya for her love and compassion.

Ritual to Return Energy and Heal the Natural Waters

One of the biggest concerns facing followers of Yemaya, and indeed, the world as a whole, is the state of the world's oceans. Plastic pollution and marine litter are threatening the world's waters at unprecedented rates. This ritual is one that is designed to provide healing energy to the natural waters of the world.

You will need the following:

- 7 shells – cowrie shells are best, but any shells work
- 7 blue and white flowers

This ritual can be conducted next to a natural body of water or in your home. If you're conducting the ritual in your home, you will also need the following:

- 1 large bowl of the freshest water possible. Distilled or spring water is ideal. Additionally, the bowl should at least be large enough for you to stand in. You can also fill a bathtub with water and immerse yourself in it.

Instructions:

1. Stand near the water (but not in it yet) and meditate on your aim for the ritual, taking the time to connect with your inner self. Think about the energy you want to share with the waters of the world and what you want to release into them.
2. Walk into the water. This is a way to physically connect to the waters of the world.
3. Call on the deities you believe in. Then, call to Yemaya and Oshun, the two Orishas associated with waters. You can also call on any other river deities that you believe in.
4. Holding the seven shells in your hand, call out to the ancestors of the shells that lived in the oceans at a time when the waters of the world were unpolluted and full of life. Ask them to bring that balance to the present so that the waters of the world can be healed.
5. Immerse the shells in the water. While you do so, say,

    "Yemaya, I offer you these shells and their ancient energy to help restore your energy, heal you, and heal the damage the world has done to you."

    Leave the shells in the water as an offering. If you're conducting the ritual at home, place them in a small bowl of salt water and place the bowl on your altar to Yemaya. Allow them to sit in the water until the full moon is over.
6. Next, take the seven flowers in your hands and call to Yemaya, Oshun, and any other water goddesses you believe in. Thank them for bringing fertility and life and giving the world the waters that nourish and cleanse all living beings. Ask the Orishas and goddesses for their blessings and ask them to help you cleanse yourself from head to foot. Feel the water moving across your feet, ankles, and the rest of your body if you are immersed in the water. Feel the cool freshness of the water, and the water helping you release everything you wish to cleanse yourself of, which will be carried away by the water.
7. Release the flowers in the water, feeling the water healing you. As you do so, thank Yemaya and the other goddesses and Orishas by saying,

"Yemaya, I offer you these flowers as thanks for your love, compassion, healing, and protection. I offer you my thanks for the waters that nourish us and the air that sustains us."

8. Take time to connect with the wisdom of Yemaya and reflect on how thankful you are for her gifts to the world. Give your thanks to the oceans and the waters of the world, as well as to Yemaya, Oshun, the other deities of water you pray to, and the ancestors.

Clean and Conserve the Waters

Aside from providing the waters of the world with healing energy, you should also take a more proactive role in helping heal the waters of the world. You can do this by looking for organizations in your area that are taking a leading role in cleaning local bodies of water.

Ask them if you can volunteer with them and help pick up trash from the waters and beaches. If there is no water body in your local area, look for organizations that are doing work protecting the water and donate time or money to helping them in any way you can.

You can also write letters to members of your government to advocate for policies that protect the waters or help out organizations that are already working on doing so. If no such organization exists in your area, you can also consider starting one yourself.

Additionally, you can take steps to conserve water where possible. Work to reduce water waste and take steps to collect and use rainwater to reduce your water usage. You can also look at the actions your area is taking to recycle wastewater and look for ways to contribute. Some steps you can take to reduce your water usage include:

- Take shorter showers or bucket baths instead of bathing in the bathtub
- Only run the washing machine when you have a full load of clothes
- Reuse greywater from your laundry in your garden
- Turn off the tap when not in use - for example, when brushing your teeth or washing fruit and vegetables
- Only run the dishwasher when you have a full load
- Use drip irrigation instead of sprinklers in your garden
- Use collected rainwater to water your garden

- Remove turf on your lawn and replace it with water-efficient plants

Conclusion

The fact that you've chosen to worship Yemaya out of every other Orisha shows that you already have a spiritual connection with her. It doesn't matter if you've not been initiated yet. You're bound to get there in no time with just a bit of practice and consistency. Hopefully, the guidance provided in this book will prove to be helpful to your practice.

Whether you choose to worship Yemoja with spells and magic or simple offerings and prayers depends completely on you. Just remember that magic, in its natural state, is everywhere. You don't have to be a uniquely special person to be able to access the magic connecting you to the Goddess of the Sea. She is indeed kind and generous to those wanting to connect with her. Similarly, whether you decide to make the charms, candles, incense, and other offerings from scratch or buy them from the market depends completely on you.

Keep in mind that the worship of an Orisha deity is deeply personal and can be unique to every individual. There are no strict rules limiting the practices carried out for their worship. There is no wrong or right way. Simply practice the way that you feel reflects your inner feelings about the goddess. This is why you'll find very few rituals that are identical. The important part is to find your own path when worshiping the Mother Goddess, Yemaya.

The path to finding Yemaya can be long and hard if you begin without any guidance. This can be especially difficult for people who do not have the same cultural heritage as people from traditional African religions. Plus, these traditions and practices are usually very secretive, making it difficult for a non-native to learn about them. While the internet is a great resource for these things, there are not enough accurately-presented sources of information about this topic. Many of the sources online are misleading, but if you are successful in finding an authentic source of information, you should never hesitate to learn more about the mystical world of the Orisha.

There is no exclusive path you need to walk on in order to reach Yemaya. She traveled around the world with Obba Nani, leaving a part of herself everywhere she went. Therefore, it's safe to assume that her blessings do not only extend to the people who are a part of her religion but also to anyone who would want to join her devotees.

Building an altar for Yemaya should be no different than for any other Orisha. Just make sure you follow the color theme associated with the goddess, as explained in the book. Moreover, the offerings and charms should also be relevant to the information provided in the book about the goddess's likes and dislikes. Finally, the prayers should be said with complete devotion, but there's no hard and fast rule about following the prayers to the word. So you can make any alterations you want.

Here's another book by Mari Silva that you might like

Your Free Gift
(only available for a limited time)

Thanks for getting this book! If you want to learn more about various spirituality topics, then join Mari Silva's community and get a free guided meditation MP3 for awakening your third eye. This guided meditation mp3 is designed to open and strengthen ones third eye so you can experience a higher state of consciousness. Simply visit the link below the image to get started.

https://spiritualityspot.com/meditation

References

Anzaldua, G. (2009). Yemayá. In A. L. Keating, W. D. Mignolo, I. Silverblatt, & S. Saldívar-Hull (Eds.), The Gloria Anzaldúa Reader (pp. 242-242). Duke University Press.

Beyer, C. (2012a, June 11). The Orishas. Learn Religions. https://www.learnreligions.com/who-are-the-orishas-95922

Beyer, C. (2012b, June 14). The Orishas: Orunla, Osain, Oshun, Oya, and Yemaya. Learn Religions. https://www.learnreligions.com/orunla-osain-oshun-oya-and-yemaya-95923

Brandon, G. (2018). orisha. In Encyclopedia Britannica.

Canson, P. E. (2014). Yemonja. In Encyclopedia Britannica.

Cuban Santeria tradition and practices. (n.d.). Anywhere.com. https://www.anywhere.com/cuba/travel-guide/santeria

Eze, C. (2022, September 25). Yoruba mythology: The Orishas of the Yoruba race. The Guardian Nigeria News - Nigeria and World News; Guardian Nigeria. https://guardian.ng/life/yoruba-mythology-the-orishas-of-the-yoruba-race/

Mark, J. J. (2021). Orisha. World History Encyclopedia. https://www.worldhistory.org/Orisha/

Merten, P. (2018, July 31). In Cuba, Santería flourishes two decades after ban was lifted. The GroundTruth Project. https://thegroundtruthproject.org/cuba-santeria-catholicism-religion-flourish-two-decades-freedom-granted/

Murphy, J. M. (1988). Santeria: An African religion in America. Beacon Press.

Rhys, D. (2020, December 1). Yemaya (yemoja) - Yoruba Queen of the sea. Symbol Sage. https://symbolsage.com/yemaya-queen-of-the-sea/

Rituals and customs. (n.d.). BBC. https://www.bbc.co.uk/religion/religions/santeria/ritesrituals/rituals.shtml

Santeria deities. (n.d.). BBC. https://www.bbc.co.uk/religion/religions/santeria/beliefs/orishas.shtml

Sawe, B. E. (2019, April 17). What is the Yoruba religion? Yoruba beliefs and origin. WorldAtlas. https://www.worldatlas.com/articles/what-is-the-yoruba-religion.html

Snider, A. C. (2019, July 9). The history of Yemaya, santeria's queenly ocean goddess mermaid. Yahoo Life. https://www.yahoo.com/lifestyle/history-yemaya-santeria-apos-queenly-144630513.html

What is Santeria? (n.d.). AboutSanteria. http://www.aboutsanteria.com/what-is-santeria.html

Wigington, P. (2011, November 15). What is Santeria? Learn Religions. https://www.learnreligions.com/about-santeria-traditions-2562543

Wigington, P. (2019, November 29). Yoruba religion: History and beliefs. Learn Religions. https://www.learnreligions.com/yoruba-religion-4777660

Yoruba. (n.d.). Everyculture.com. https://www.everyculture.com/wc/Mauritania-to-Nigeria/Yoruba.html

Yoruba creation myth. (n.d.). Gateway-africa.com. https://www.gateway-africa.com/stories/Yoruba_Creation_Myth.html

(N.d.). Teenvogue.com. https://www.teenvogue.com/story/the-history-of-yemaya-goddess-mermaid

Amata. (2016, August 5). Sacred stories of the Orishas. Journey of a 21st Century Afrikan Queen. https://giramatans.wordpress.com/2016/08/05/sacred-stories-of-the-orishas/

Control of the seasons in the new kingdom - The Yoruba Religious Concepts. (n.d.). Google.com. https://sites.google.com/site/theyorubareligiousconcepts/control-of-the-seasons-in-the-new-kingdom

Goddess wisdom: Yemaya's story. (2013, July 18). Self-Love Rainbow; Blessing Manifesting. https://www.selfloverainbow.com/2013/07/goddess-wisdom-yemayas-story.html

Importance of mythology. (n.d.). Prezi.com. https://prezi.com/remyxkfdbc4o/importance-of-mythology/

In Search of Myths & Heroes. What is a Myth? (n.d.). Pbs.org. https://www.pbs.org/mythsandheroes/myths_what.html

Marriage of Oba Nani and Shango - the Yoruba Religious concepts. (n.d.). Google.com. https://sites.google.com/site/theyorubareligiousconcepts/marriage-of-oba-nani-and-shango

Rhys, D. (2020a, December 1). Olokun – Orisha of the depths of the ocean. Symbol Sage. https://symbolsage.com/olokun-sprit-of-waters/

Rhys, D. (2020b, December 1). Yemaya (yemoja) – Yoruba Queen of the sea. Symbol Sage. https://symbolsage.com/yemaya-queen-of-the-sea/

The separation of Oya and Yemaya - The Yoruba Religious Concepts. (n.d.). Google.com. https://sites.google.com/site/theyorubareligiousconcepts/marriage-of-oba-nani-and-shango/the-separation-of-oya-and-yemaya-1

Turnbull, L. (2022, October 28). Yemaya, the Santeria goddess of the ocean. Goddess Gift; The Goddess Path. https://goddessgift.com/goddesses/yemaya/

Yemaya abandons Arganyu in Oshuns Ile - The Yoruba Religious Concepts. (n.d.). Google.com. https://sites.google.com/site/theyorubareligiousconcepts/yemaya-abandons-arganyu-in-oshuns-ile

Yemaya becomes the Apetebi (woman) of Orula - The Yoruba Religious Concepts. (n.d.). Google.com. https://sites.google.com/site/theyorubareligiousconcepts/yemaya-becomes-the-apetebi-woman-of-orula-1

Yemaya offers Oshun marriage with Arganyu - The Yoruba Religious Concepts. (n.d.). Google.com. https://sites.google.com/site/theyorubareligiousconcepts/yemaya-offers-oshun-marriage-with-arganyu

Beyer, C. (n.d.). Syncretism - What Is Syncretism? Learn Religions. https://www.learnreligions.com/what-is-syncretism-p2-95858

Snider, A. C. (2019, July 9). The History of Yemaya, Santeria's Queenly Ocean Goddess Mermaid. Teen Vogue. https://www.teenvogue.com/story/the-history-of-yemaya-goddess-mermaid

Viarnés, C. (n.d.). All Roads Lead to Yemayá: Transformative Trajectories in the Procession at Regla. Hemisphericinstitute.Org. https://hemisphericinstitute.org/en/emisferica-5-1-traveling/5-1-essays/all-roads-lead-to-yemaya-transformative-trajectories-in-the-procession-at-regla.html

Gardner, L. (2009, September 29). Cult of the Saints: An Introduction to Santeria. Llewellyn Worldwide. https://www.llewellyn.com/journal/article/2048

Chai, S. C. (2021, November 9). The Virgin Mary and Blue: What is the Significance? – F O R M F L U E N T. F O R M F L U E N T. https://formfluent.com/blog/the-virgin-mary-and-blue-what-is-the-significance

Dorsey, L. (2015, September 7). How to create A sacred space for Yemaya. Voodoo Universe. https://www.patheos.com/blogs/voodoouniverse/2015/09/how-to-create-a-sacred-space-yemaya/

Jorgenson, J. (2019, July 13). Exploring the yorùbá goddess Yemaya. Exemplore. https://exemplore.com/wicca-witchcraft/Exploring-the-Yorb-Goddess-Yemaya

Kaufman, A. (2022, September 3). How to connect with Yemaya? Goddess Yemaya altar setup, offerings, & more. Digest From Experts. https://digestfromexperts.com/4361/how-to-connect-with-yemaya-altar-offerings/

Prayers for Yemaya - powerful & uplifting words for prayer. (n.d.). Prayerist.com. https://prayerist.com/prayer/yemaya

Toni. (2019, February 14). Connecting with Yemaya - . In the Key of Soul. https://www.inthekeyofsoul.com/mainblog/yemaya

Zeeshan. (2022, January 30). How to connect with Yemaya. Digital Global Times. https://digitalglobaltimes.com/how-to-connect-with-yemaya/

Morgaine, R. (2021). Yemaya: Orisha, Goddess, and Queen of the Sea. Weiser Books.

Kaufman, A. (2022, September 3). How To Connect With Yemaya? Goddess Yemaya Altar Setup, Offerings, & More. Digest From Experts. https://digestfromexperts.com/4361/how-to-connect-with-yemaya-altar-offerings/

Quinn, A. (2018, September 28). Life-Changing Benefits of Home Shrines. Abbeygale Quinn. https://abbeygalequinn.com/benefits-of-home-shrines/

Creating an Orisha Altar. (n.d.). Original Botanica. https://originalbotanica.com/blog/creating-an-orisha-altar-

Learning to Surrender: The Sacred Lessons of Yemayá. Atmos. https://atmos.earth/ocean-conservation-santeria-yemaya-lessons/

PURIFICATION BATHS WITH YEMAYA. (2021, May 20). BOTANICA OCHUN. https://botanicaochunco.com/purification-baths-with-yemaya/

Gomez, A. R. (2010, March 29). Spell: Yemaya Bath Ritual. Llewellyn Worldwide. https://www.llewellyn.com/spell.php?spell_id=4038

Nana. (2014, December 7). BIGGEST SECRET ON YEMAYA LOVE SPELL REVEALED. TRUTH. Love Spells. https://lovespell.tips/yemaya-spells-for-love-that-works/

Crawshaw, E. (2021, October 26). 8 Spells and Rituals for Self-Love. Mysticum Luna. https://mysticumluna.com/blogs/blog/10-spells-and-rituals-for-self-love

Amogunla, F. (2020, December 6). Dance, water, and prayers: Celebrating the goddess Yemoja. Al Jazeera. https://www.aljazeera.com/features/2020/12/6/dance-water-and-prayers-celebrating-the-goddess-yemoja

Celebrating Yemaya: The mother of the ocean and sea in African diasporic traditions. (n.d.). Daily Kos.

https://www.dailykos.com/stories/2022/7/10/2108414/-Celebrating-Yemaya-The-mother-of-the-ocean-and-sea-in-African-diasporic-traditions

Grimond, G. (2017, June 30). Brazil's goddess of the sea: Everything you need to know about festival of Iemanjá. Culture Trip; The Culture Trip. https://theculturetrip.com/south-america/brazil/articles/brazils-goddess-of-the-sea-everything-you-need-to-know-about-festival-of-iemanja/

Slama, F. (2020, January 23). Iemanjá Festival. Salvador - Bahia - Mix It Up. https://www.salvadordabahia.com/en/iemanja-festival/

Zelenková, B. (n.d.). Iemanja: A Uruguayan celebration of the Yoruba goddess of the sea. Ethnologist.Info. https://ethnologist.info/2019/04/25/iemanja-a-uruguayan-celebration-of-the-yoruba-goddess-of-the-sea/

A ritual to Yemaya – mother whose children are the fish. (2018, January 31). Judith Shaw - Life on the Edge. https://judithshaw.wordpress.com/2018/01/31/a-ritual-to-yemaya-mother-whose-children-are-the-fish/

Atmos. (2022, June 21). Learning to surrender: The sacred lessons of Yemayá. Atmos. https://atmos.earth/ocean-conservation-santeria-yemaya-lessons/

Celebrant Institute. (2011, December 23). A goddess water ritual for new year's eve. Spirituality & Health. https://www.spiritualityhealth.com/blogs/spirituality-health/2011/12/23/celebrant-institute-goddess-water-ritual-new-years-eve

Episode 51- Yemaya, the Yoruba Orisha "mother of all" – part 2 of seashells and ocean goddesses. (n.d.). Moonriverrituals.com. https://moonriverrituals.com/episode-51-yemaya-the-yoruba-orisha-mother-of-all-part-2-of-seashells-and-ocean-goddesses/

Original Products. (2018, December 31). Yemaya: The goddess of the New Year. Original Botanica; www.originalbotanica.com#creator. https://originalbotanica.com/blog/yemaya-the-goddess-of-the-new-year

Ratcliffe, D. (2017, June 7). A healing ritual for Yemaya (and YOU) on World Oceans Day. Inner Journey Events Blog. https://innerjourneyevents.wordpress.com/2017/06/07/a-healing-ritual-for-yemaya-and-you-on-world-oceans-day/

Reduce water consumption at home. (2012, January 24). Sswm.Info; seecon international gmbh. https://sswm.info/taxonomy/term/2658/reduce-water-consumption-at-home

Yemanja feast day: Uruguans flock to the beach to pay ode to sea goddess. (n.d.). https://www.outlookindia.com/ . Retrieved November 28, 2022, from https://www.outlookindia.com/international/yemanja-feast-day-uruguans-flock-to-the-beach-to-pay-ode-to-sea-goddess-photos-66798?photo-1

www.ingramcontent.com/pod-product-compliance
Lightning Source LLC
Chambersburg PA
CBHW051846160426
43209CB00006B/1183